VOL. 14

HAL•LEONARD®
GUITAR PLAY-ALONG

AUDIO ACCESS INCLUDED

BLUES ROCK

CONTENTS

PLAYBACK+
Speed • Pitch • Balance • Loop

To access audio visit:
www.halleonard.com/mylibrary

5646-2951-4972-9467

Tracking, mixing, and mastering by Jake Johnson
All guitars by Doug Boduch
Bass by Tom McGirr
Keyboards by Warren Wiegratz
Drums by Scott Schroedl

ISBN 978-0-634-05634-5

Visit Hal Leonard Online at
www.halleonard.com

HAL•LEONARD®
7777 W. BLUEMOUND RD. P.O. BOX 13819
MILWAUKEE, WISCONSIN 53213

Blue on Black

Words and Music by Tia Sillers, Mark Selby and Kenny Wayne Shepherd

Drop D tuning:
(low to high) D-A-D-G-B-E

Intro

Moderately slow ♩ = 78

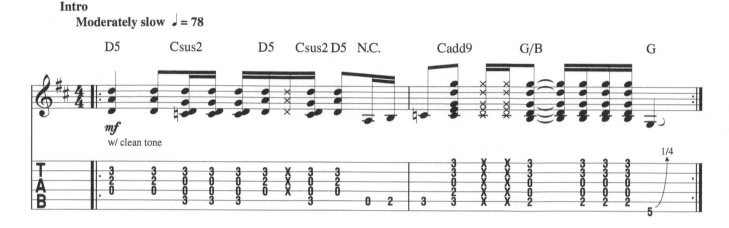

Verse

2nd time, substitue Fill 1

1. Night __ falls _____ and I'm a - lone. _____
2. *See additional lyrics*

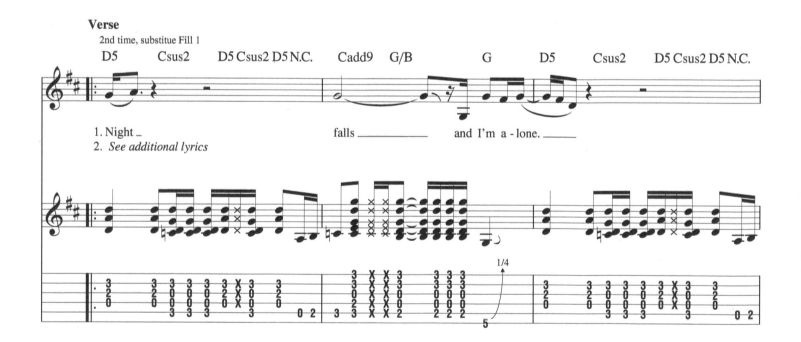

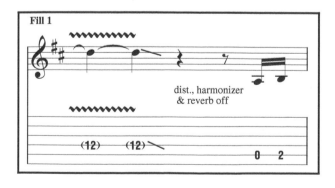

Fill 1

dist., harmonizer
& reverb off

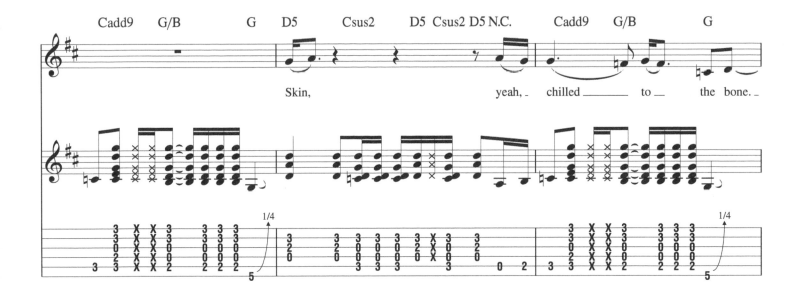

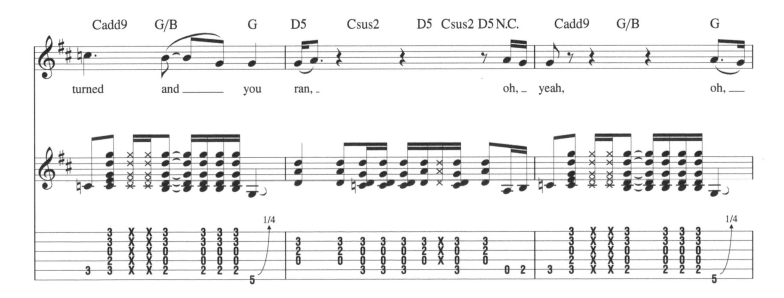

Chorus

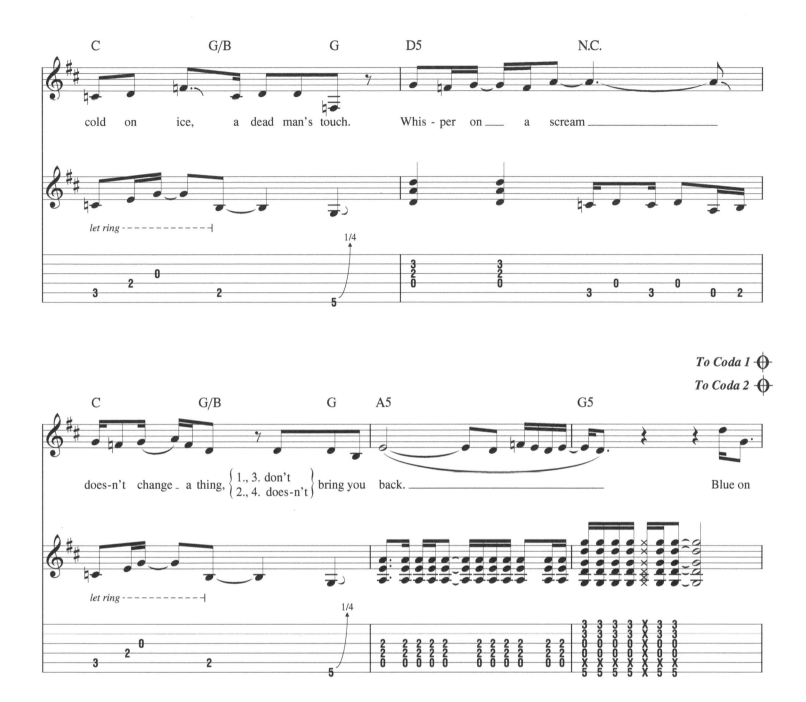

To Coda 1 ⊕
To Coda 2 ⊕

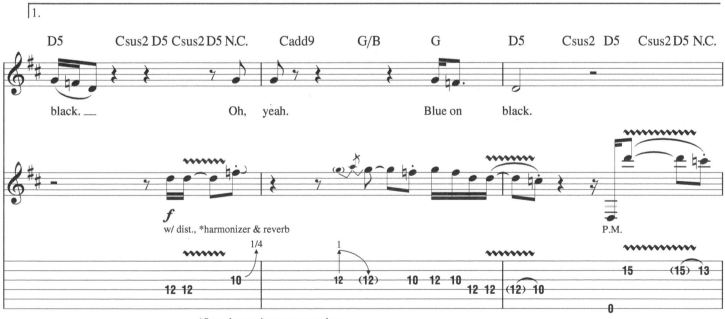

*Set to harmonize one octave above.

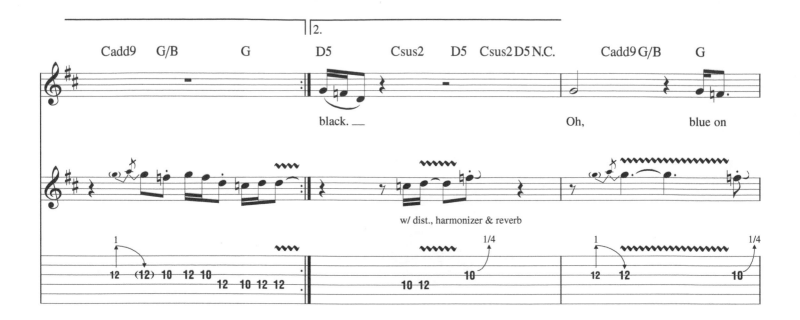

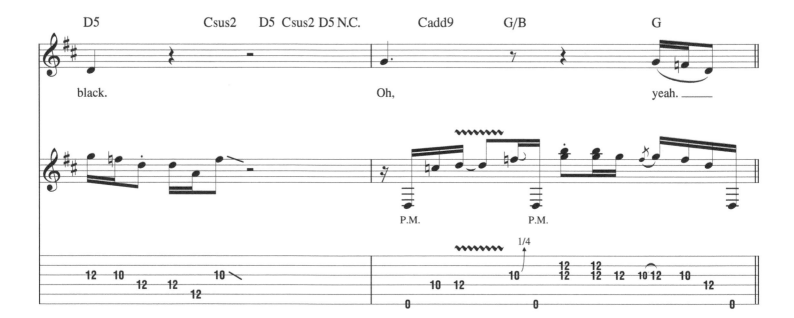

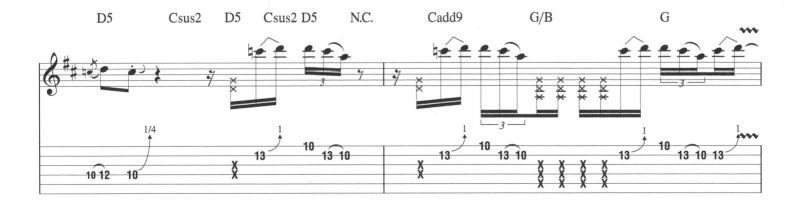

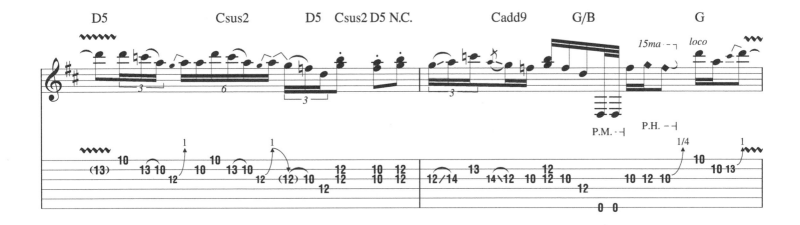

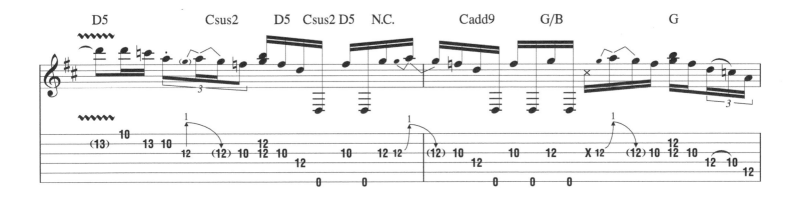

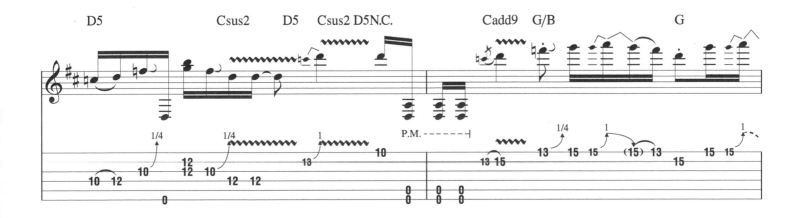

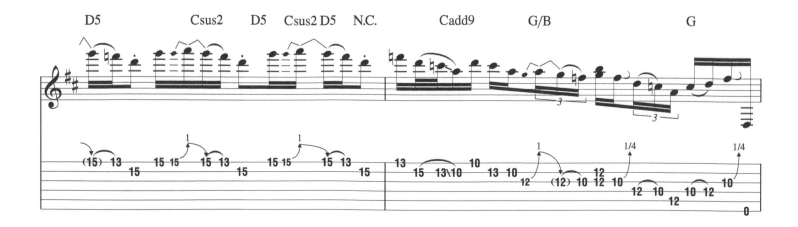

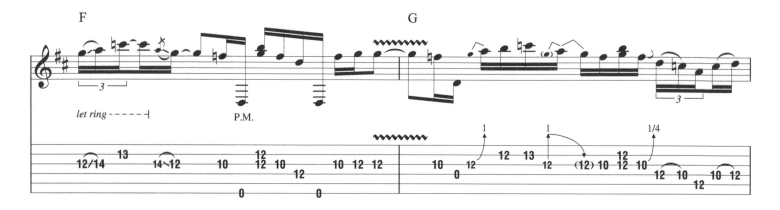

D.S. al Coda 1

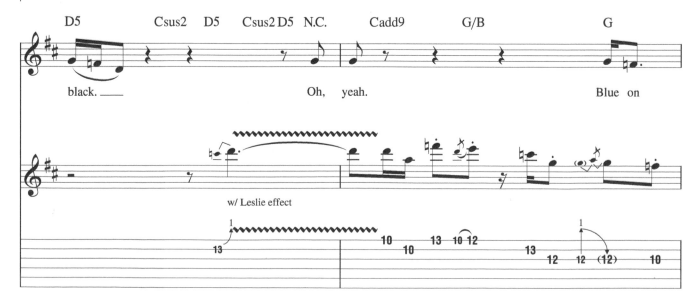

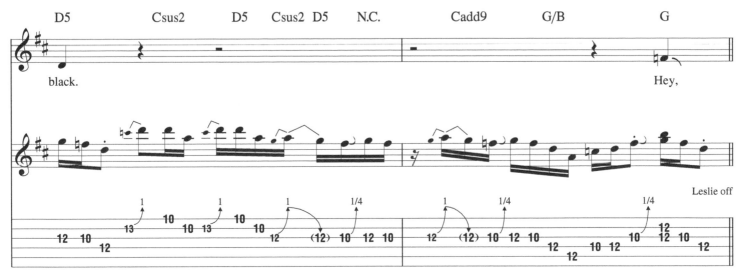

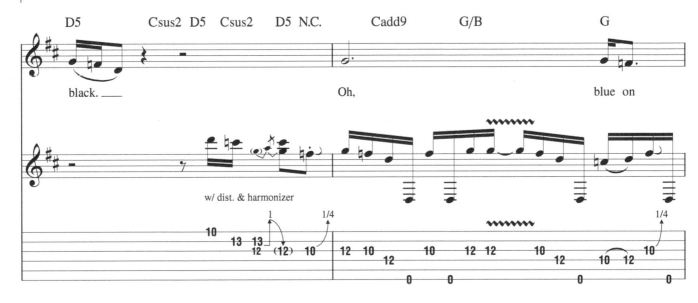

Coda 2

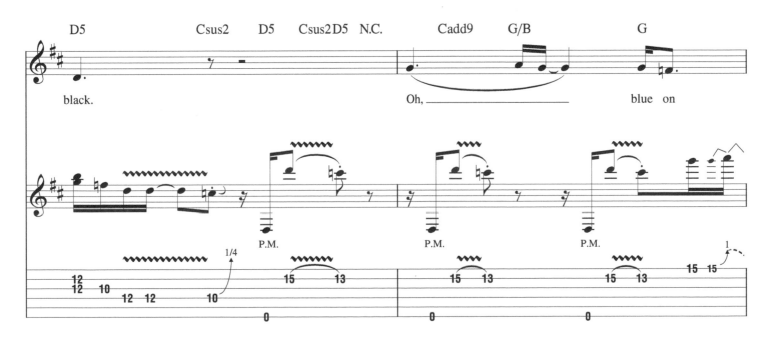

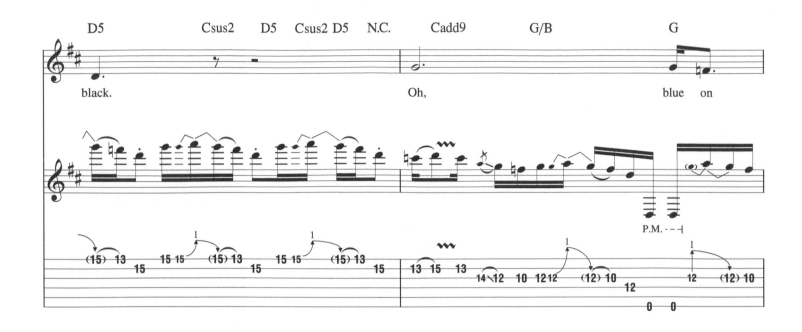

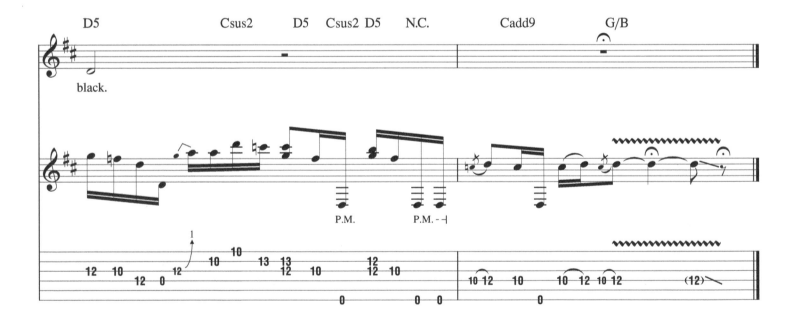

Additional Lyrics

2. Blind, oh, and now I see
Truth, lies and in between.
Wrong can't be undone.
Oh, slipped from the tip of your tongue.

Crossfire

Written by Bill Carter, Ruth Ellsworth, Reese Wynans, Tommy Shannon and Chris Layton

Tune down 1/2 step:
(low to high) Eb-Ab-Db-Gb-Bb-Eb

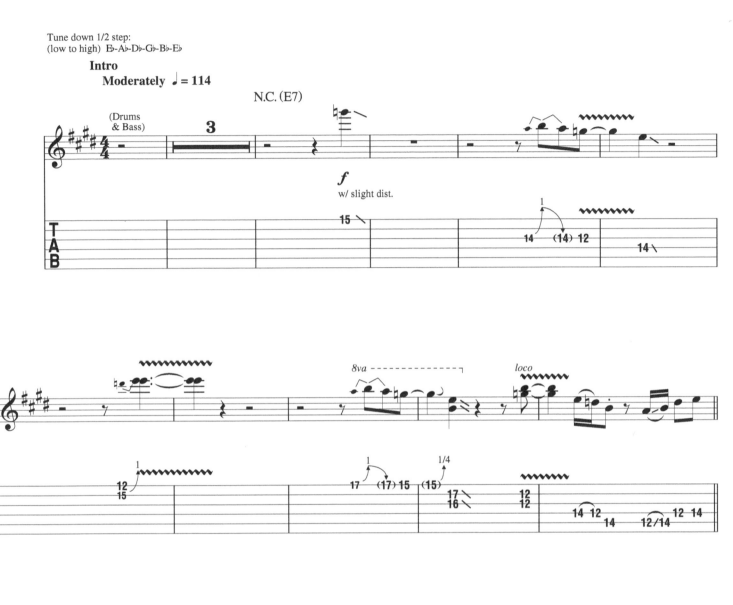

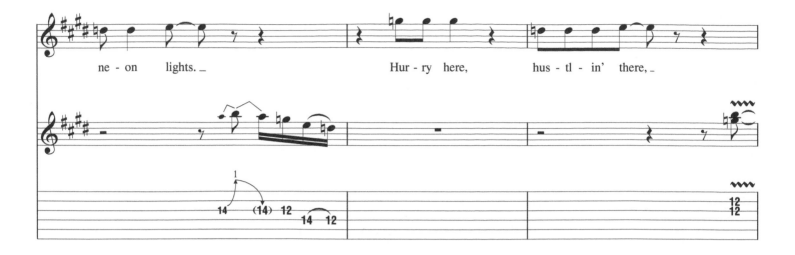

ne - on lights. _ Hur - ry here, hus - tl - in' there, _

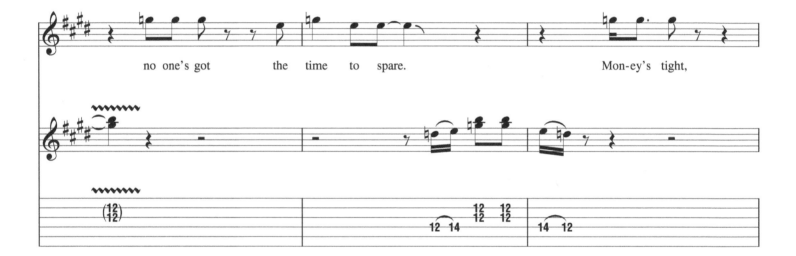

no one's got the time to spare. Mon-ey's tight,

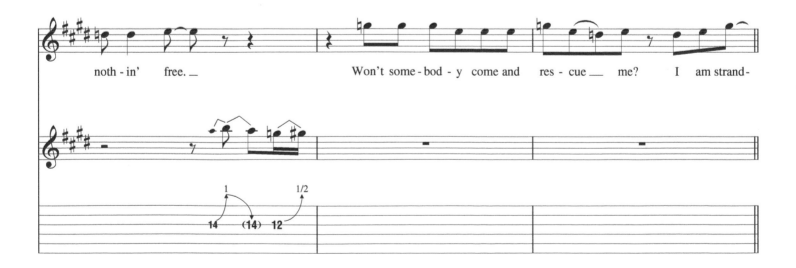

noth - in' free. _ Won't some-bod - y come and res - cue _ me? I am strand-

Chorus

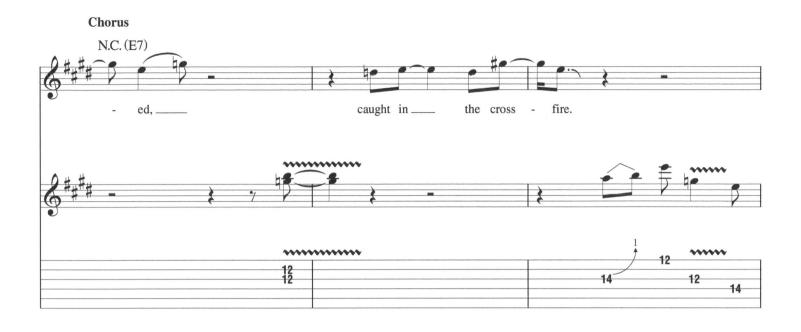

-ed, _____ caught in ____ the cross - fire.

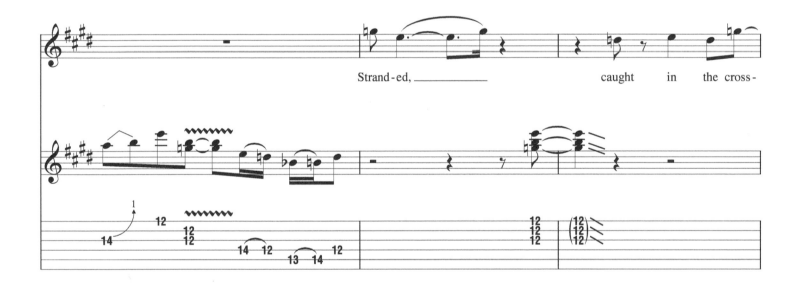

Strand-ed, _____ caught in the cross-

Verse

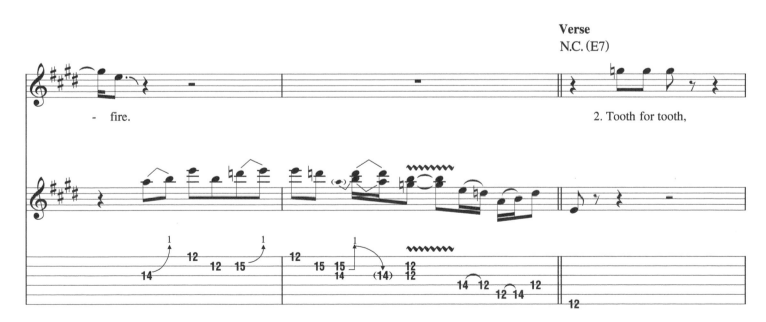

-fire. 2. Tooth for tooth,

eye for an eye, _____ sell your soul just to buy, buy, __ buy. ___

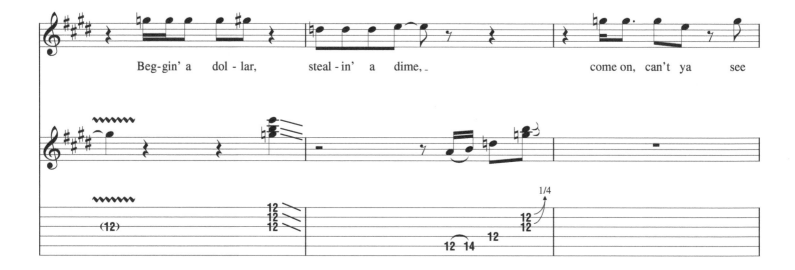

Beg-gin' a dol - lar, steal - in' a dime, __ come on, can't ya see

Chorus
N.C. (E7)

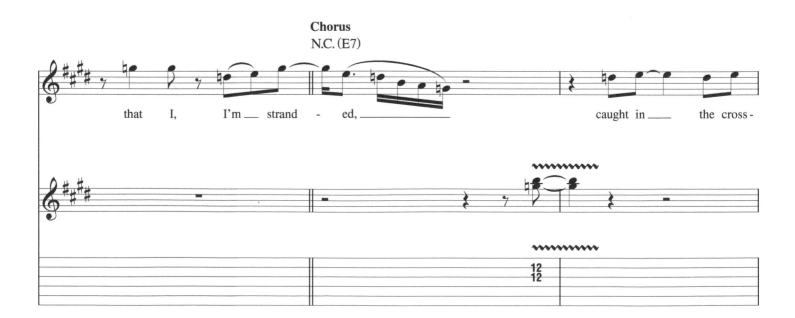

that I, I'm __ strand - ed, _____ caught in ___ the cross-

fire?

I am strand - ed,

caught in the cross - fire.

let ring - - -

Bridge

N.C. (G7)　　　　　　　　(A7)　　　　　　　　(G7)

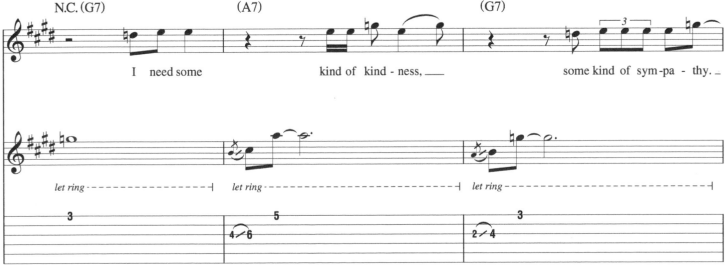

I need some　　kind of kind - ness, ____　　some kind of sym-pa - thy. __

let ring - - - - - - - - - - - - - - - - - -　　let ring -　　let ring -

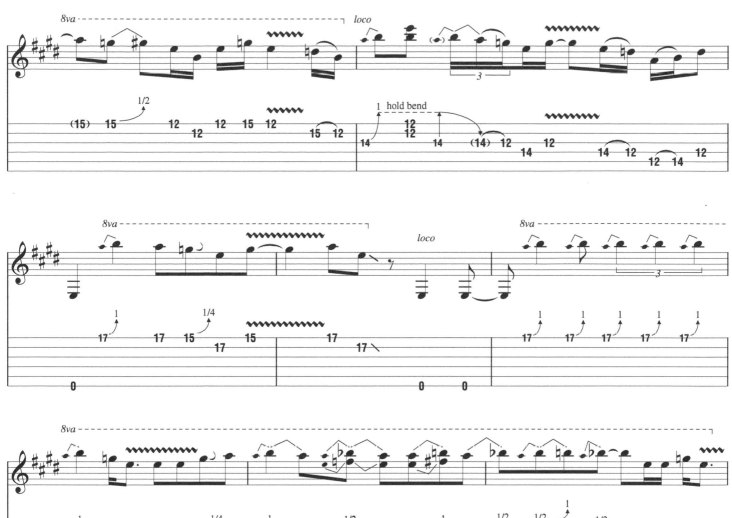

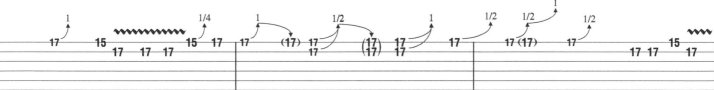

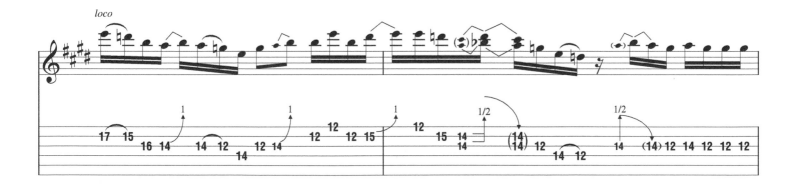

(G7)　　　　　　　　　　　(A7)　　　　　　　　(G7)

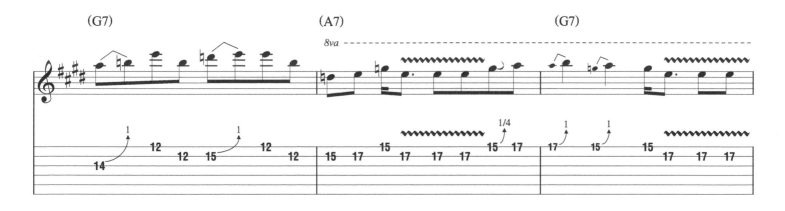

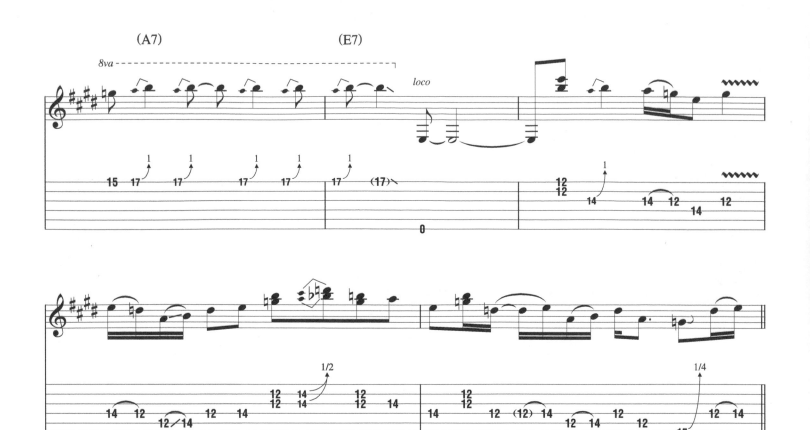

Verse

N.C.(E7)

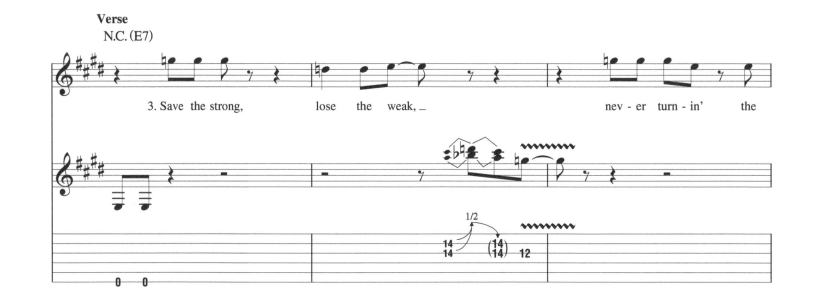

3. Save the strong,   lose the weak, _   nev - er turn - in'   the

oth - er cheek. _   Trust no - bod - y,   don't be no fool. _

Chorus
N.C. (E7)

What-ev-er hap-pened to the gold-en rule? We got strand - ed,

caught in _____ the cross - fire. We got strand-

- ed, _____ caught in _____ the cross - fire.

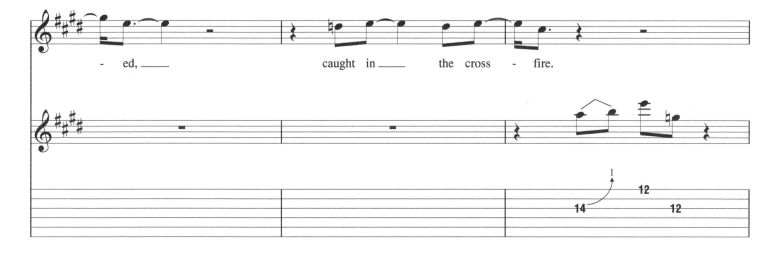

We got strand - ed,_____ caught in the cross-

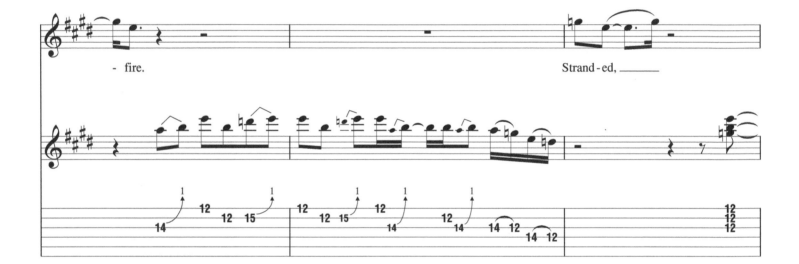

- fire. Strand - ed,_____

caught in____ the cross - fire. Help me!

Outro-Guitar Solo

N.C. (E7)

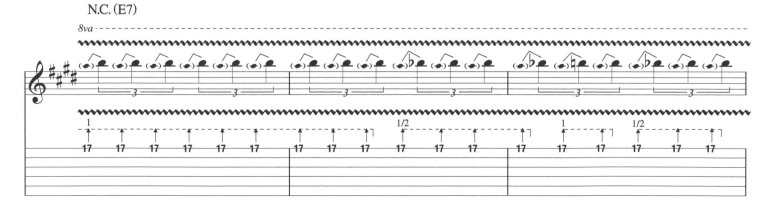

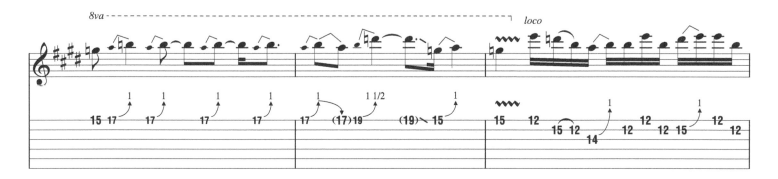

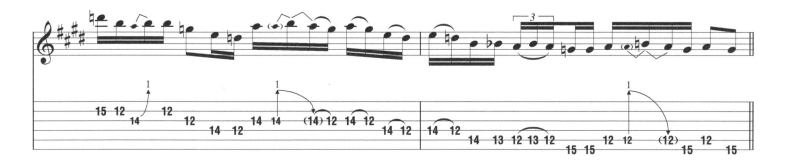

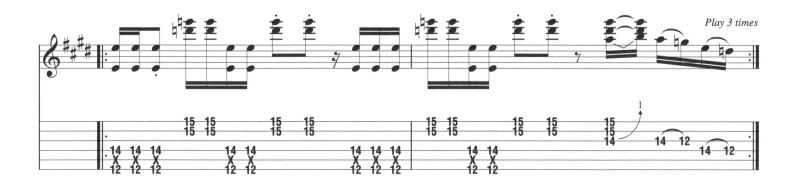

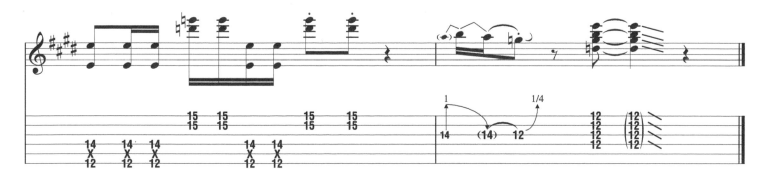

Cross Road Blues
(Crossroads)

Words and Music by Robert Johnson

Intro
Moderately fast Rock ♩ = 130

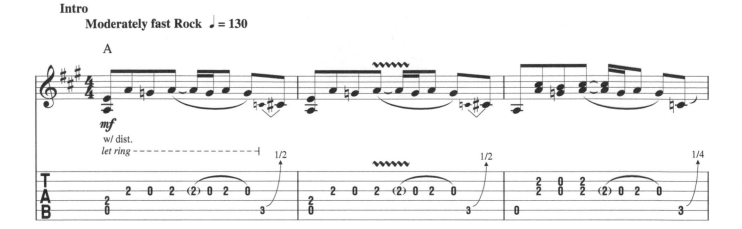

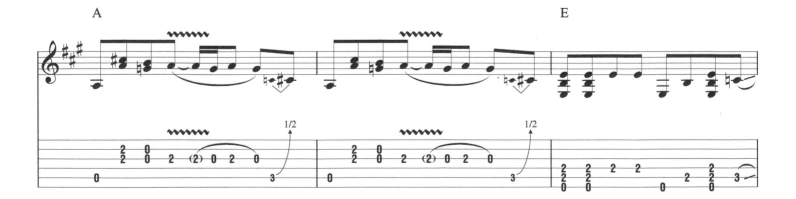

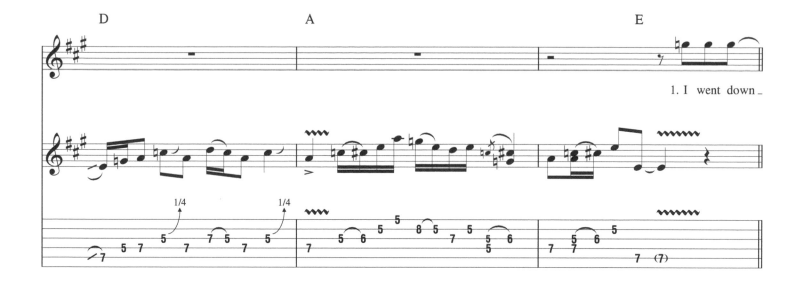

1. I went down

𝄋 Verse

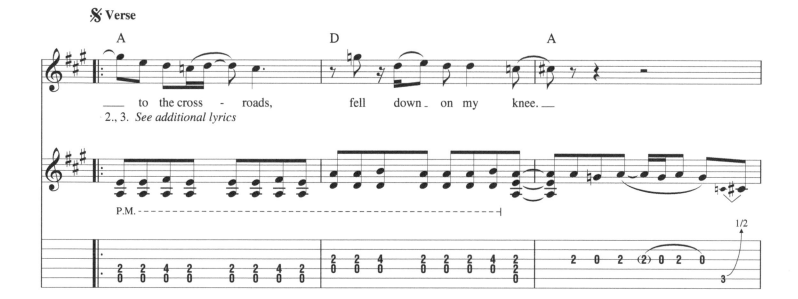

to the cross - roads, fell down on my knee.

2., 3. *See additional lyrics*

Down to the cross - roads, fell down on my knee.

Guitar Solo

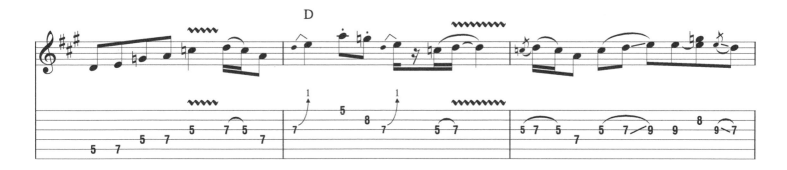

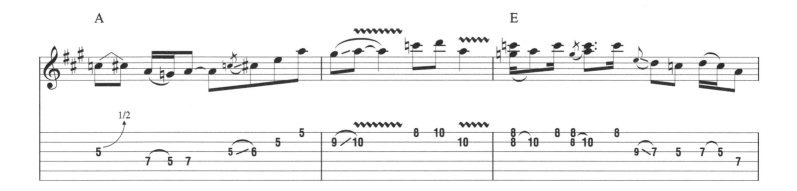

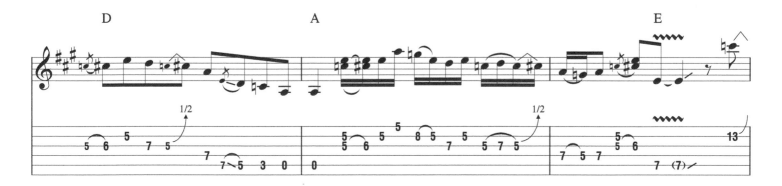

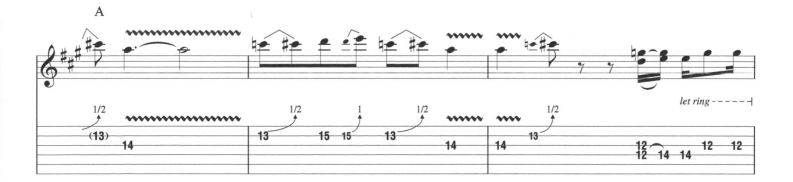

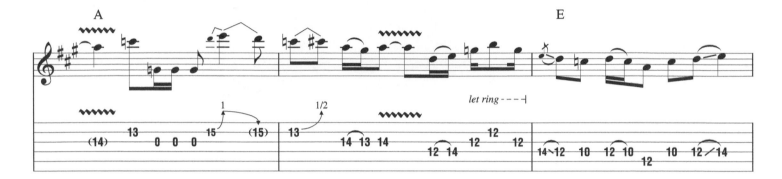

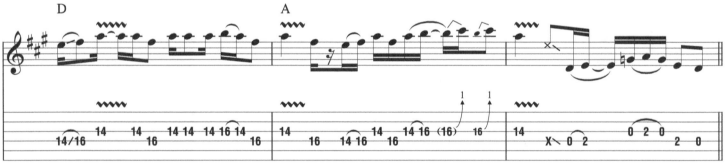

D.S. al Coda
(3rd Verse, 3rd ending)

⊕ Coda

Guitar Solo

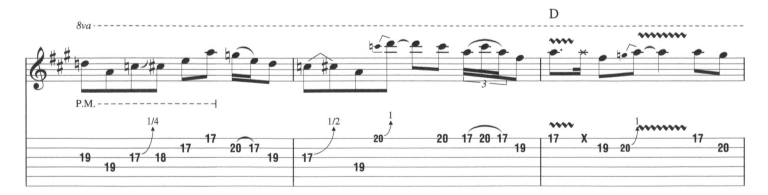

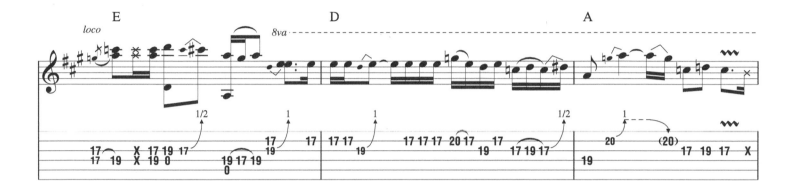

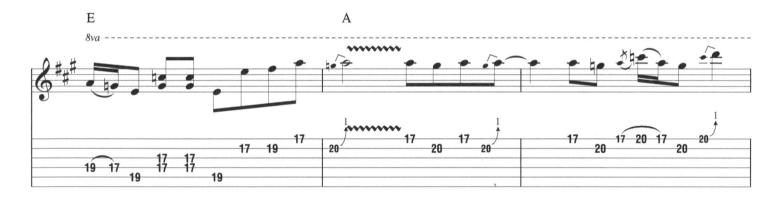

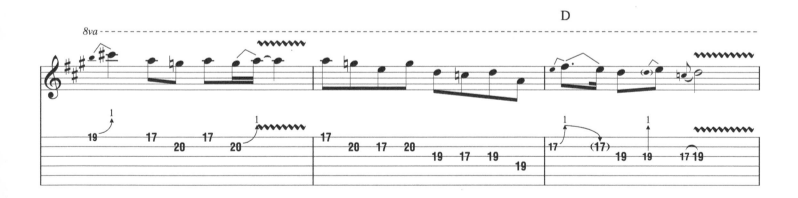

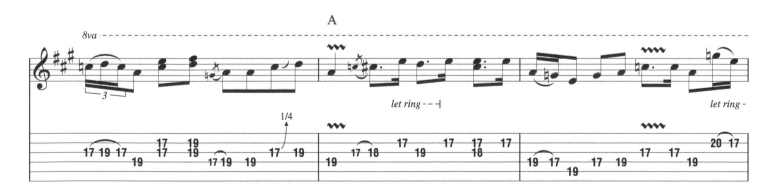

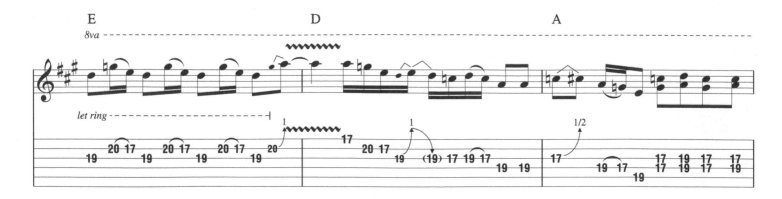

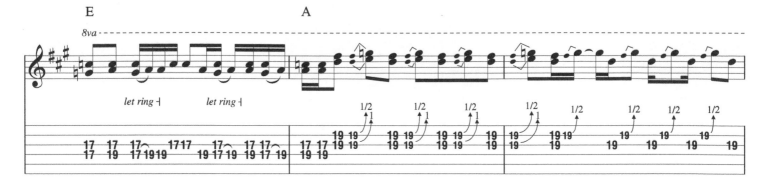

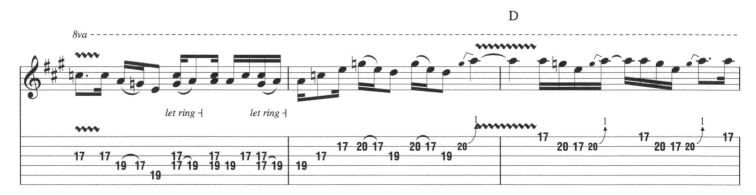

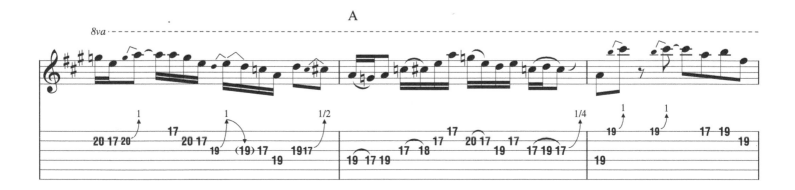

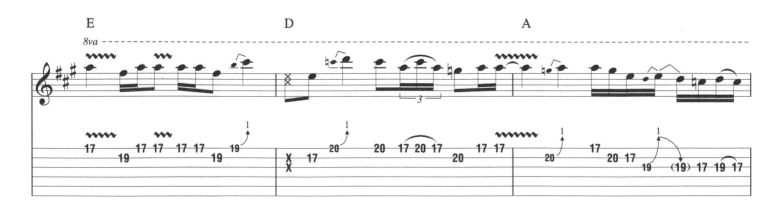

Outro-Verse

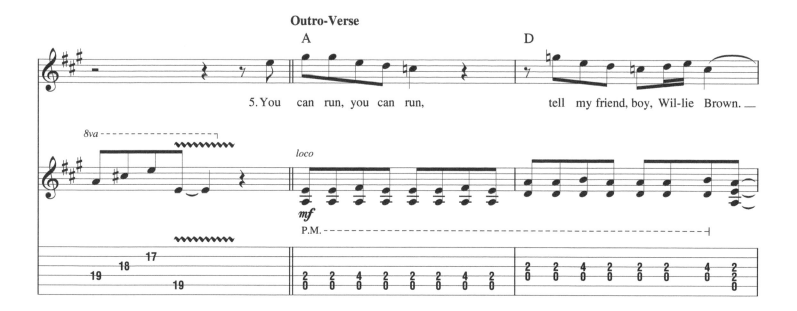

5. You can run, you can run, tell my friend, boy, Wil-lie Brown. —

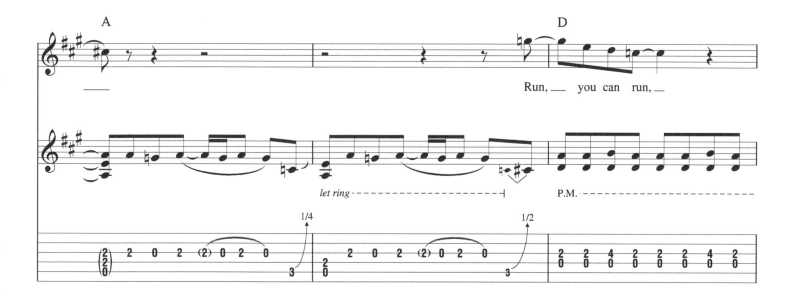

Run, — you can run,

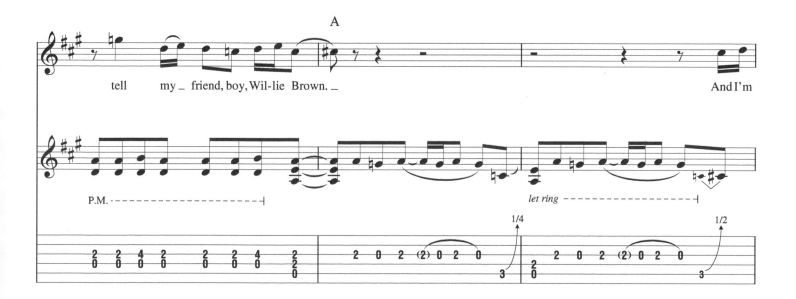

tell my _ friend, boy, Wil-lie Brown. — And I'm

stand-in' at the cross - road, be - lieve I'm__ sink - in' down.

Free time

Additional Lyrics

2. I went down to the crossroad, tried to flag a ride.
   Down to the crossroad, tried to flag a ride.
   Nobody seemed to know me. Ev'rybody passed me by.

3. When I'm goin' down to Rosedale, take my rider by my side.
   Goin' down to Rosedale, take my rider by my side.
   We can still barrelhouse, baby, on the riverside.

The House Is Rockin'

Written by Stevie Ray Vaughan and Doyle Bramhall

Tune down 1/2 step:
(low to high) Eb-Ab-Db-Gb-Bb-Eb

Intro
Fast Rock ♩ = 172

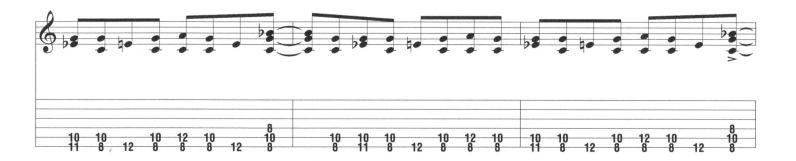

Well, ___ the house is a rock-in', but don't___

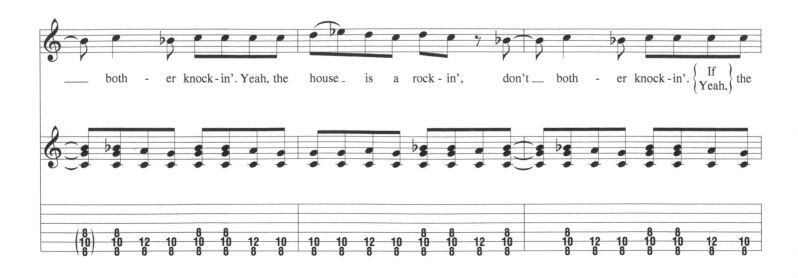

both - er knock - in'. Yeah, the house __ is a rock - in', don't __ both - er knock - in'. { If / Yeah, } the

G7   C7

house __ is a rock - in', don't _____ both - er, come on ___ in. ____

Verse
C7

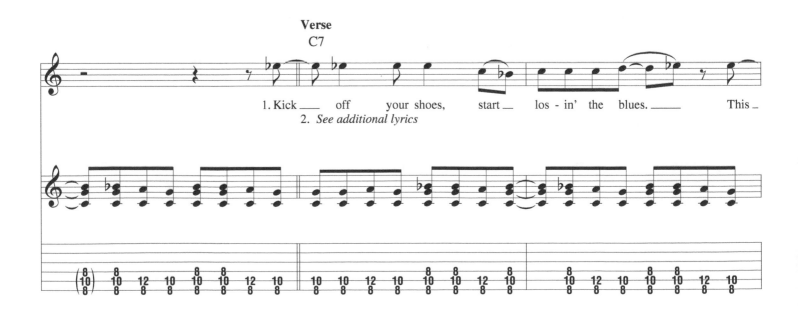

1. Kick ___ off   your shoes,   start ___ los - in' the blues. _____ This __
2. *See additional lyrics*

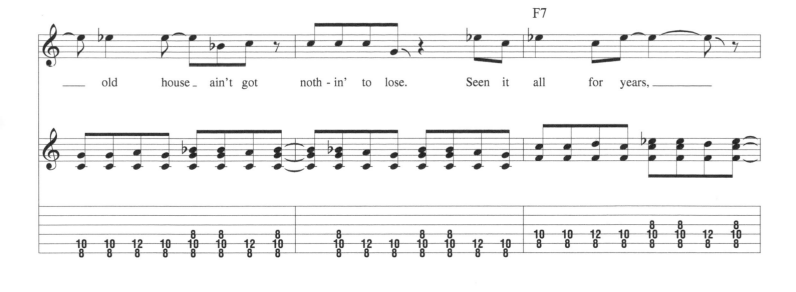

_____ old house_____ ain't got noth-in' to lose. Seen it all for years, _____

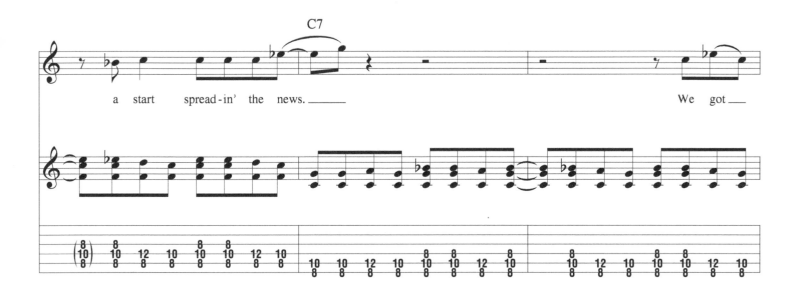

a start spread-in' the news. _____ We got _____

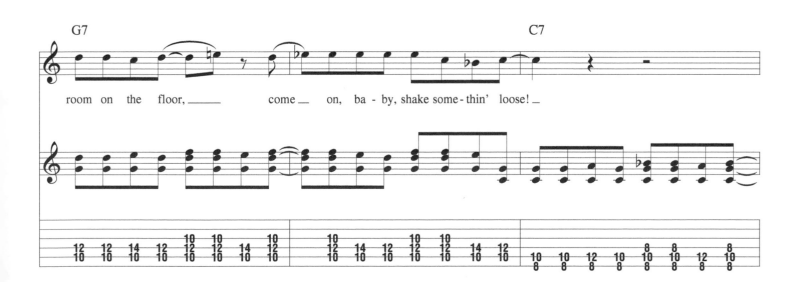

room on the floor, _____ come_____ on, ba-by, shake some-thin' loose! _____

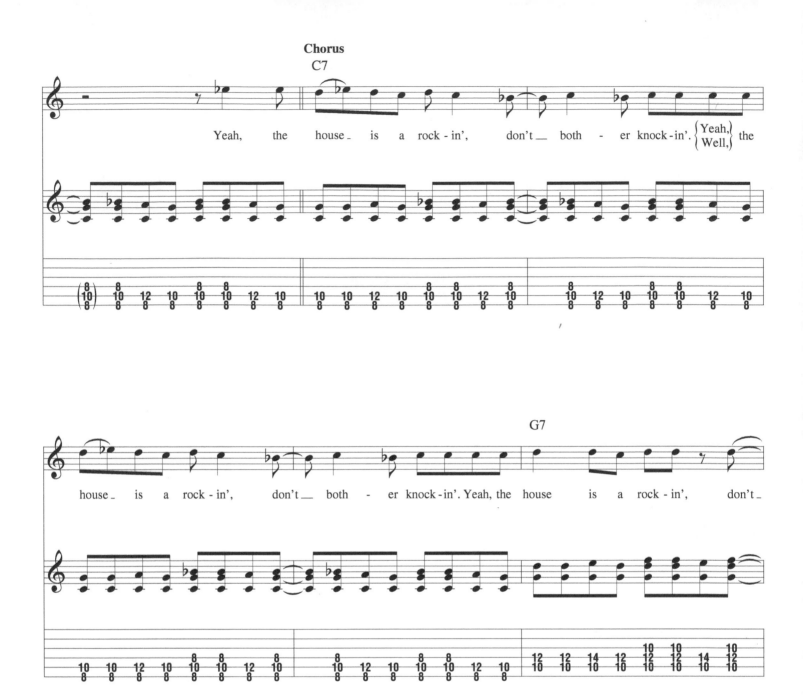

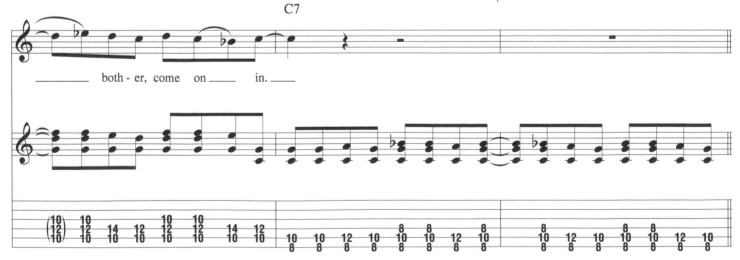

Piano Solo

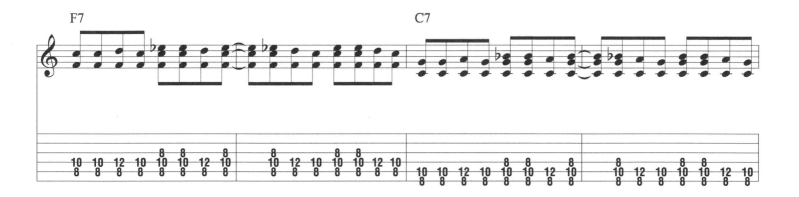

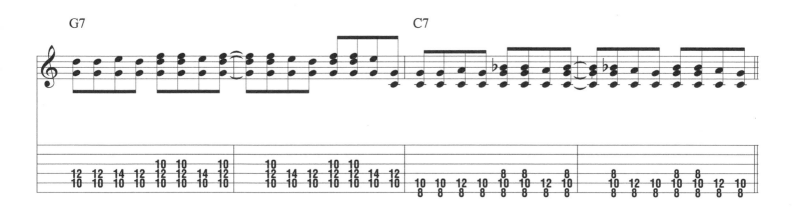

Guitar Solo

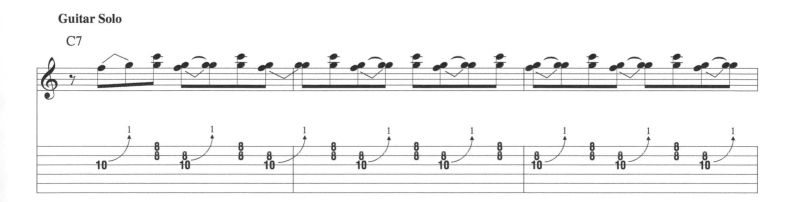

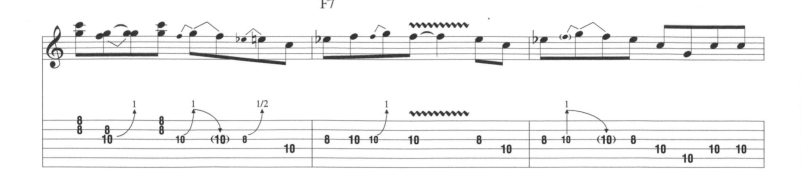

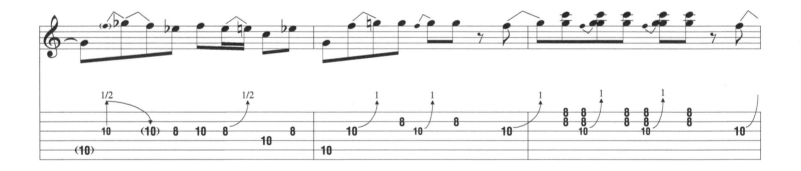

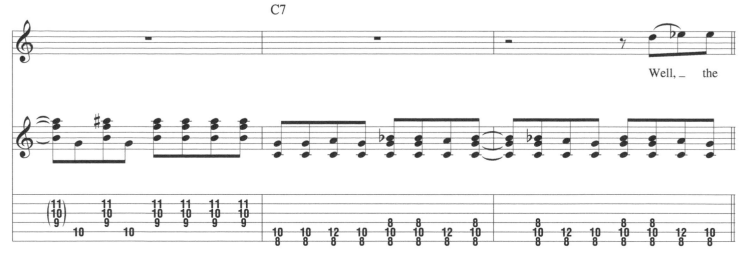

Coda

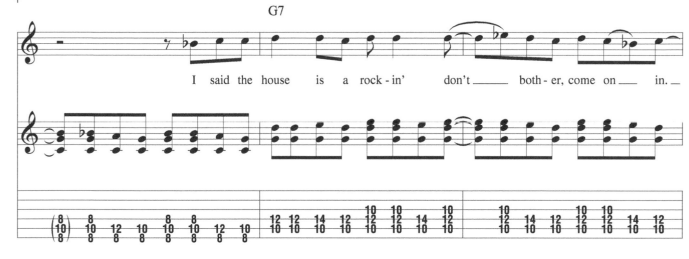

I said the house is a rock-in' don't _____ both-er, come on _____ in. _____

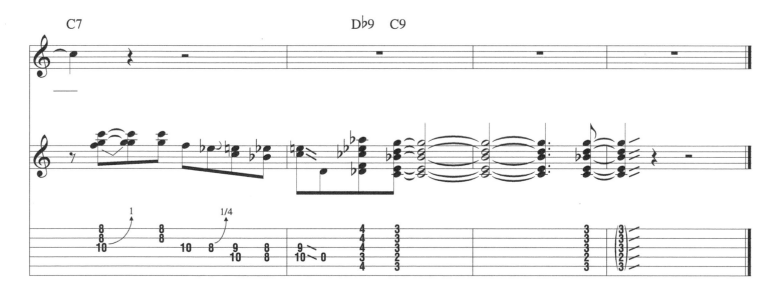

Additional Lyrics

2. Walkin' up the street, you can hear the sound
Of some bad honky tonkers really layin' it down.
They've seen it all for years, they got nothin' to lose.
So get out on the floor, shimmy till you shake somethin' loose!

La Grange

Words and Music by Billy F Gibbons, Dusty Hill and Frank Lee Beard

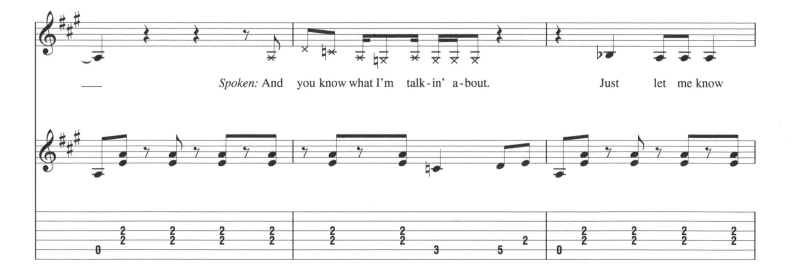

Spoken: And you know what I'm talk-in' a-bout. Just let me know

if you __ wan-na go __ to that

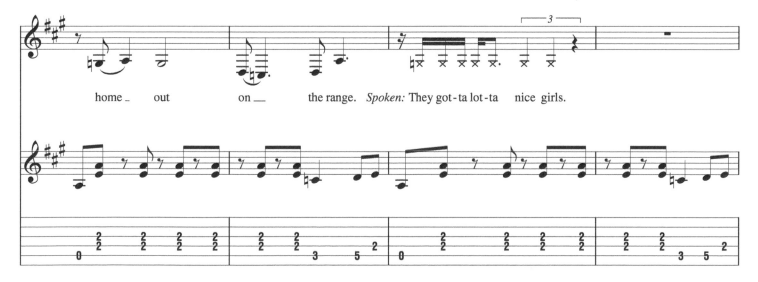

home __ out on __ the range. Spoken: They got-ta lot-ta nice girls.

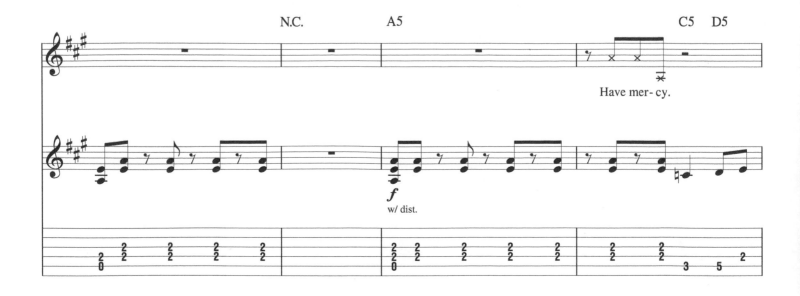

and the ten to get your - self in

a, hmm, hmm. And I hear it's tight most ev - er - y night, __

but now __ I might be mis - tak - en. __

Guitar Solo

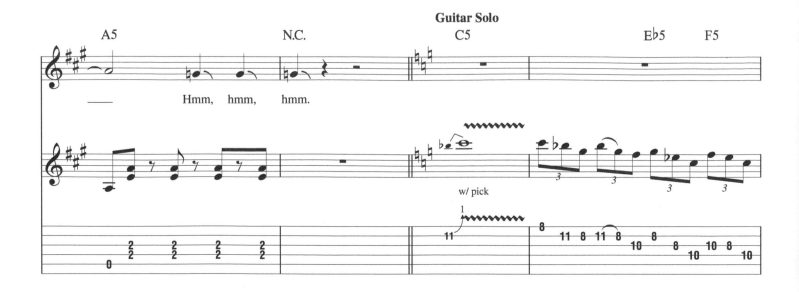

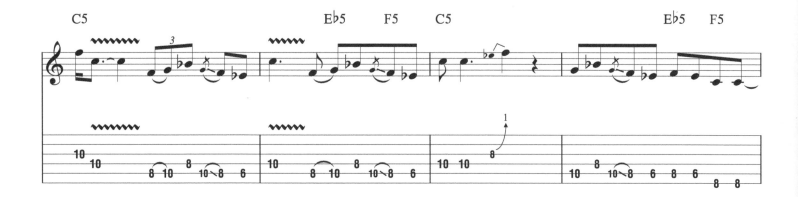

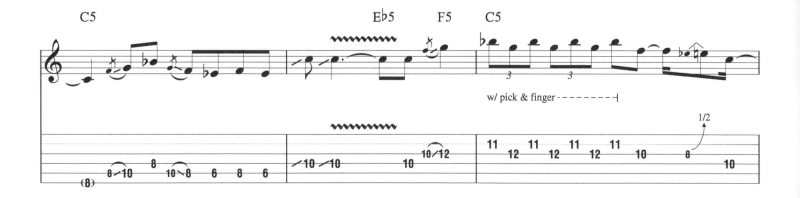

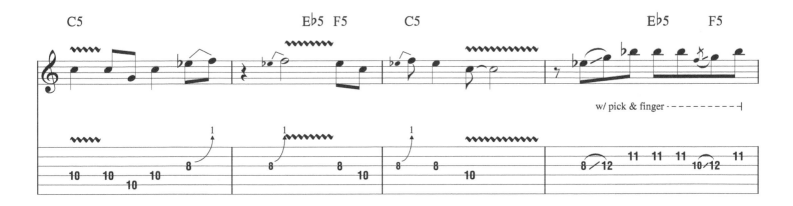

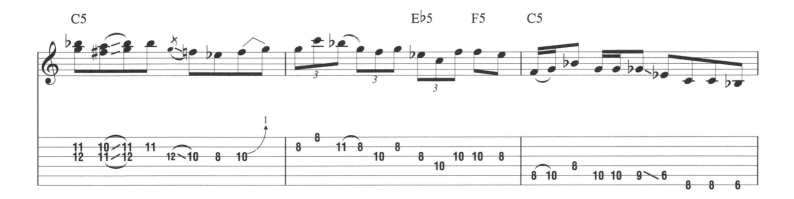

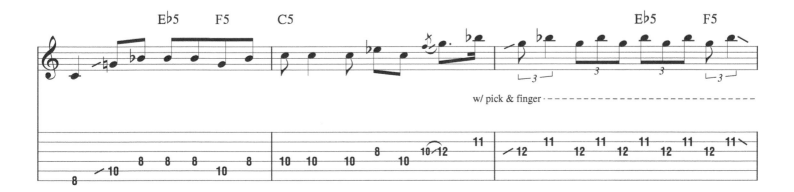

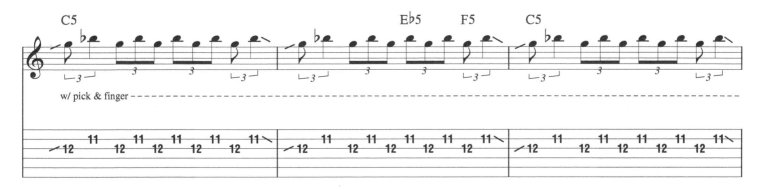

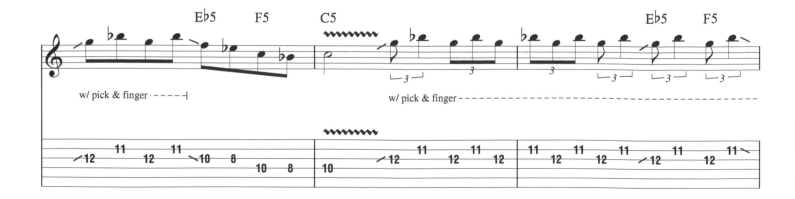

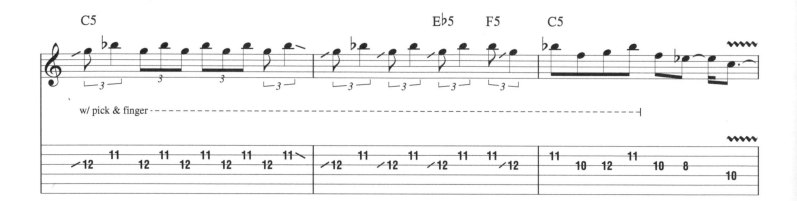

Interlude

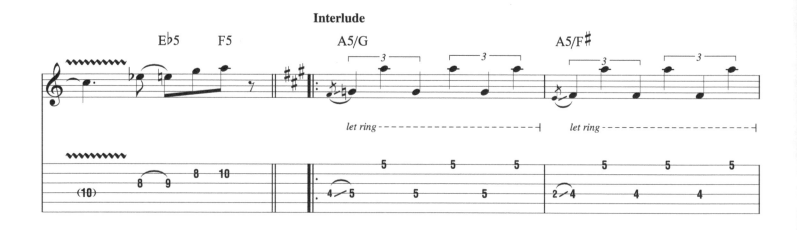

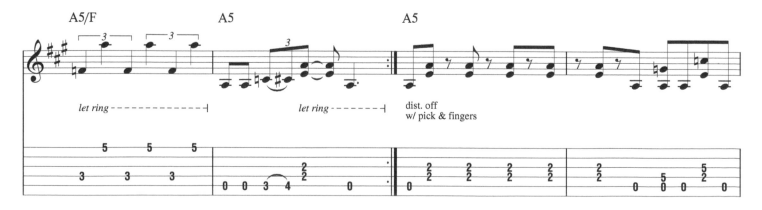

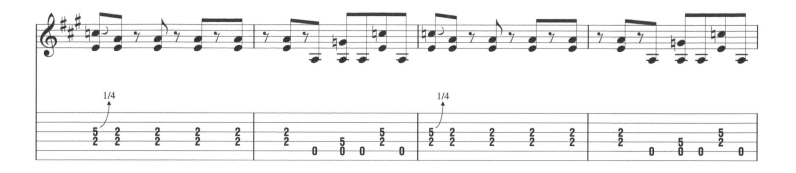

Outro-Guitar Solo

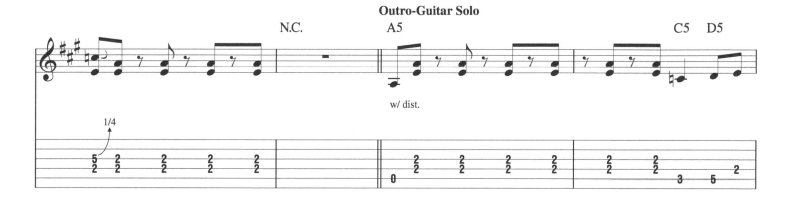

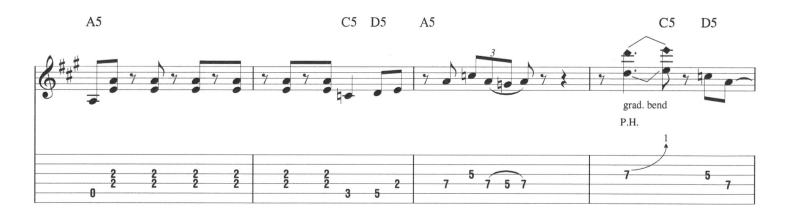

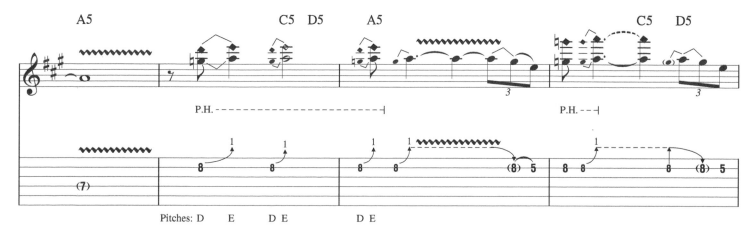

Pitches: D E   D E   D E

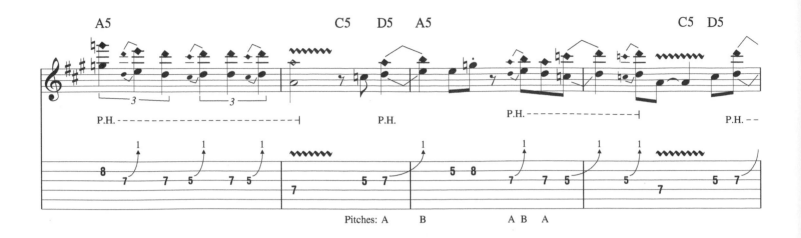

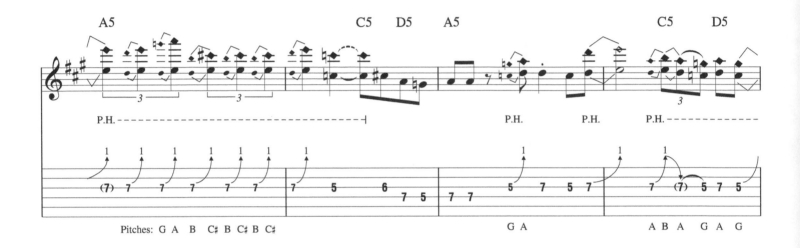

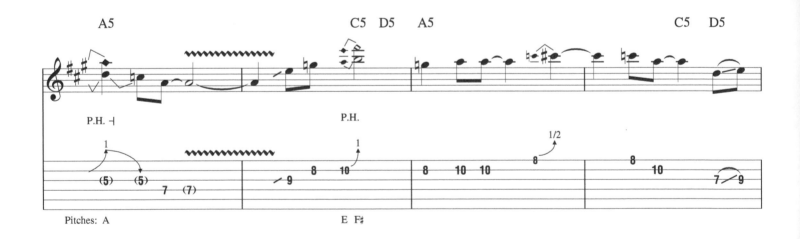

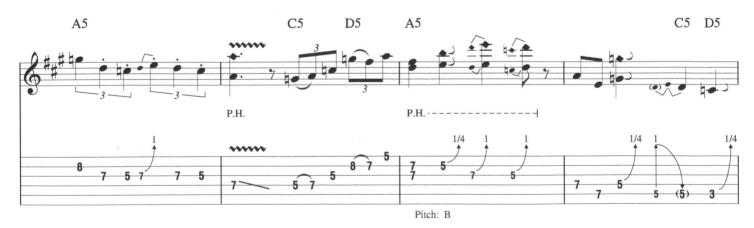

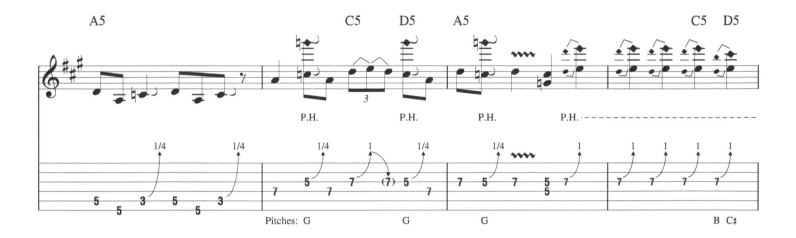

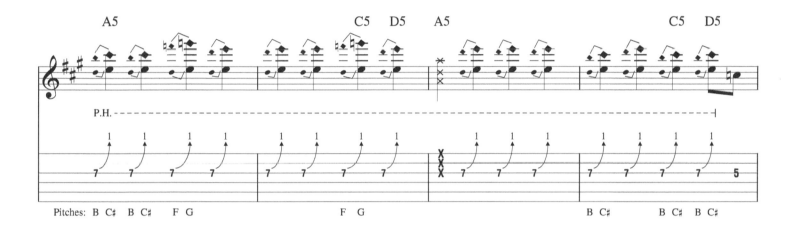

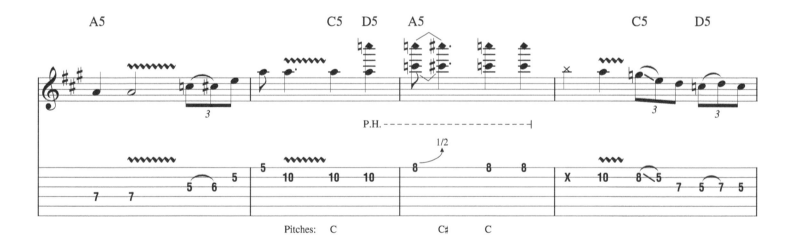

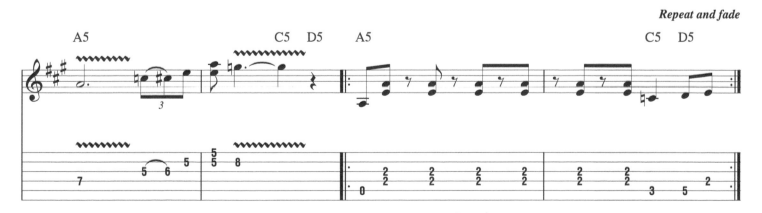

Move It on Over

Words and Music by Hank Williams

Open G tuning:
(low to high) D-G-D-G-B-D

𝄋 **Verse**

Moderate Shuffle ♩ = 147

1. I come in last night a-bout a half past ten. That ba-by of mine would-n't
2., 3., 5. *See additional lyrics*

mf
w/ slight dist.
let ring throughout

let me in. So move it on o-ver,

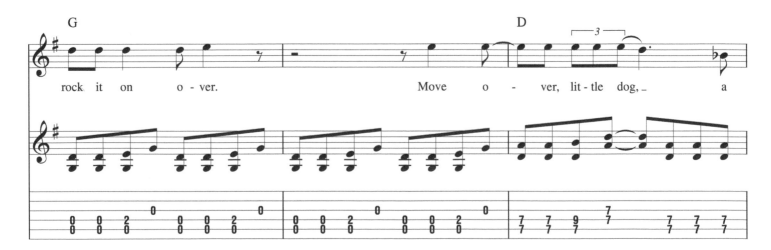

rock it on o-ver. Move o-ver, lit-tle dog, a

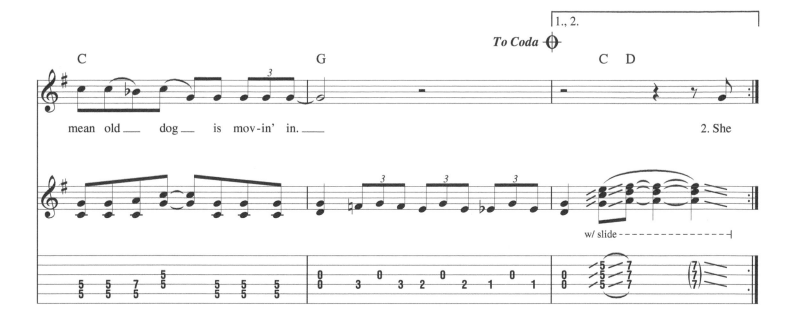

mean old __ dog __ is mov-in' in. __

2. She

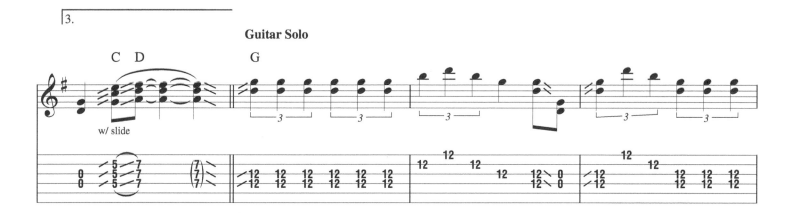

Guitar Solo

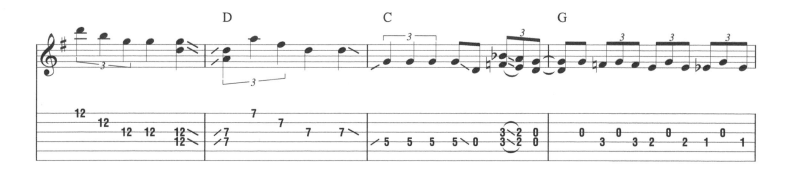

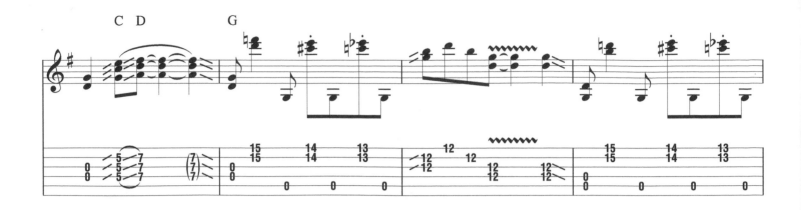

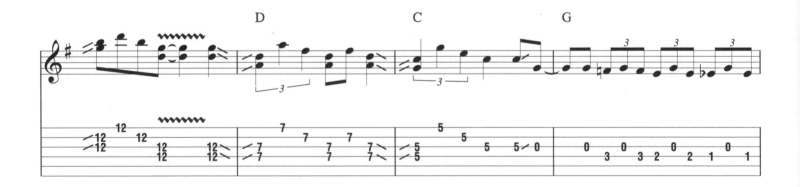

4. She threw me out ___ just as pret-ty as she please. ___

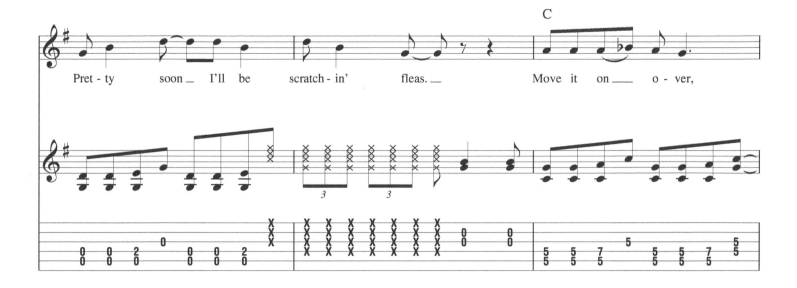

Pret - ty   soon __ I'll be scratch - in'   fleas. __   Move it on __ o - ver,

slide it on o - ver.   Move o -

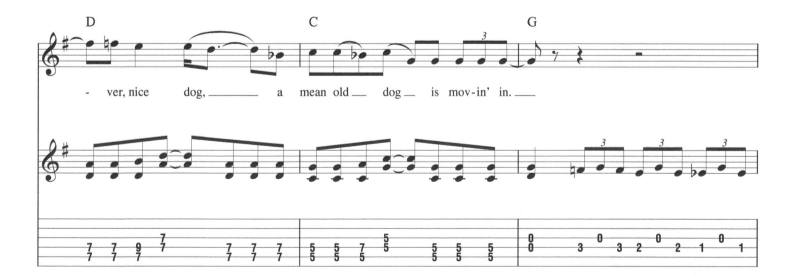

- ver, nice dog, _____ a mean old __ dog __ is mov-in' in. __

Guitar Solo

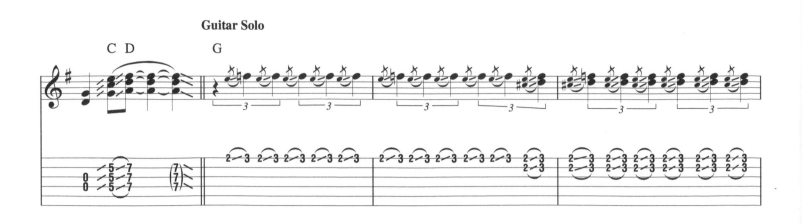

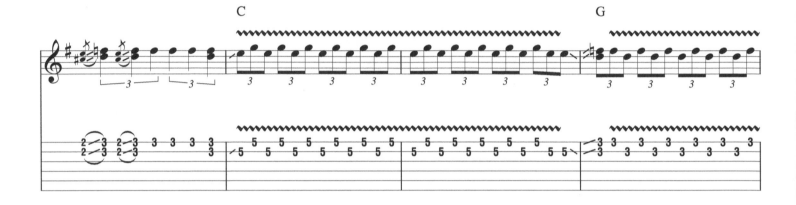

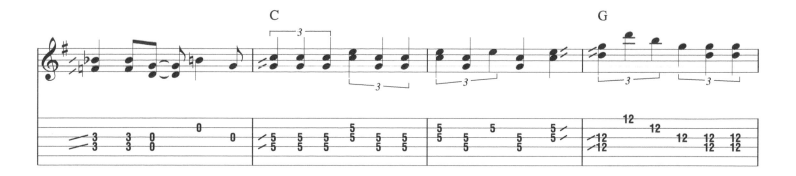

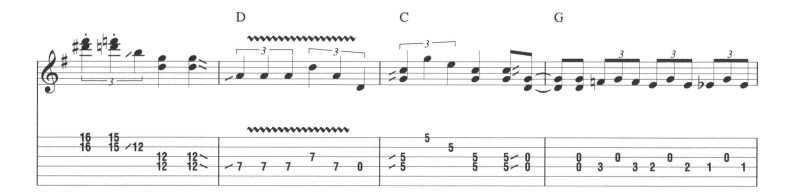

D.S. al Coda   **⊕ Coda**

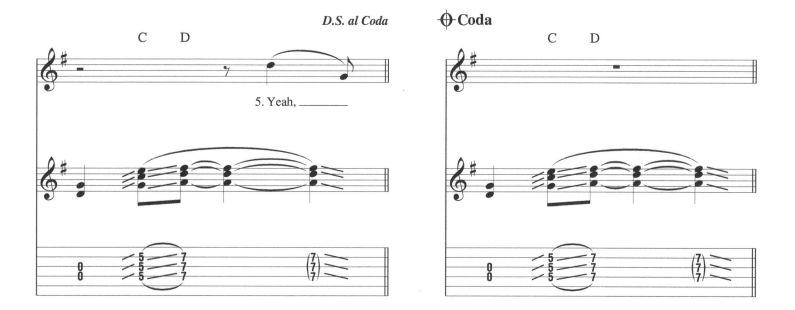

5. Yeah, _____

Guitar Solo

w/o slide

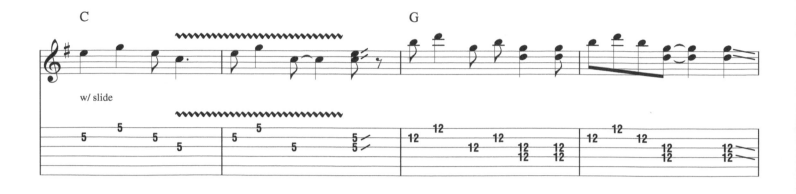

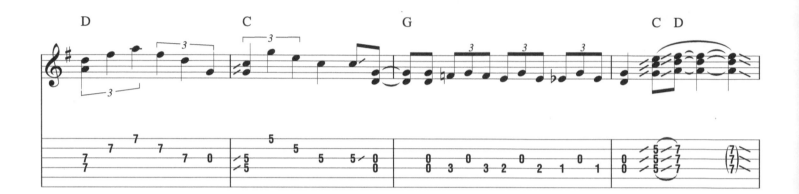

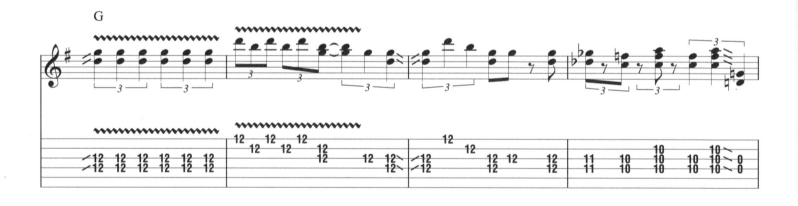

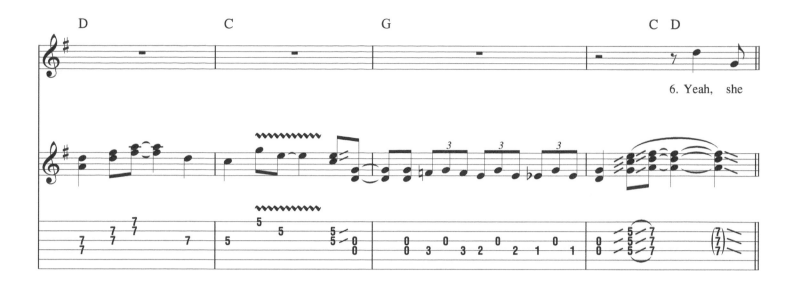

6. Yeah, she

Verse

changed the lock __ on __ my back door. Now my key, __ it won't fit no more. Move __

__ it on __ o-ver, rock it on o-ver. Move o-

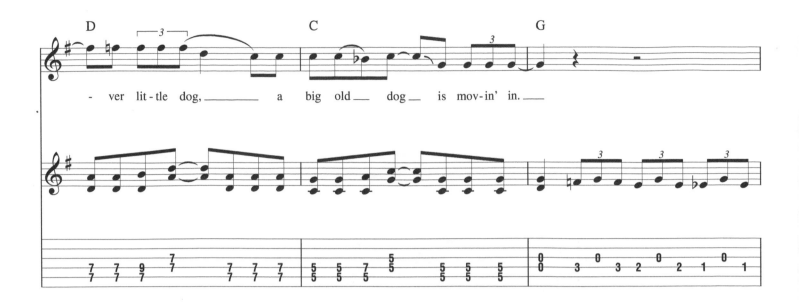

-ver lit-tle dog, _____ a big old_____ dog_____ is mov-in' in. _____

Verse

7. Move it on _____ o - ver,

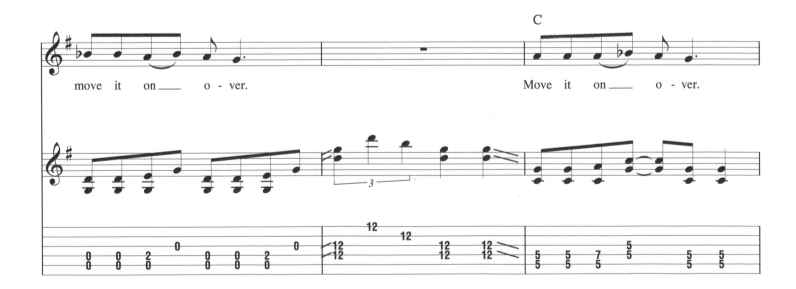

move it on _____ o - ver.

Move it on _____ o - ver.

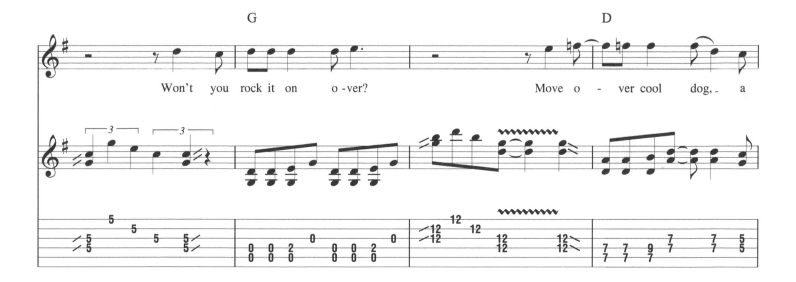

Won't you rock it on o-ver? Move o - ver cool dog, a

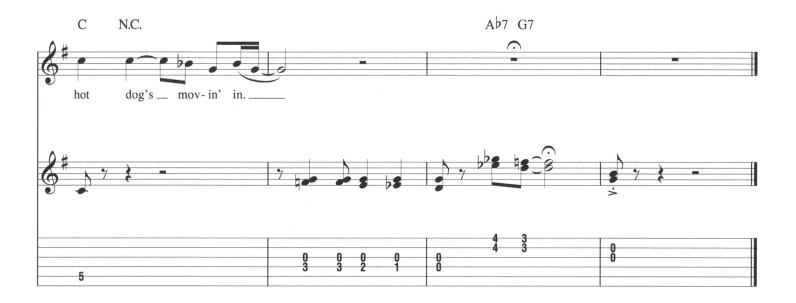

hot dog's mov-in' in.

Additional Lyrics

2. She told me not to mess around,
   But I done let the deal go down.
   Move it on over, rock it on over.
   Move over, nice dog, a big bad dog is movin' in.

3. She changed the lock on my back door.
   Now my key, it won't fit no more.
   Move it on over, rock it on over.
   Move over nice dog, a mean old dog is movin' in.

5. Yeah, listen to me, dog, before you start to whine.
   That side's your's and this side's mine.
   So move it on over, rock it on over.
   Move over little dog, a big old dog is movin' in.

Roadhouse Blues

Words and Music by The Doors

Intro
Moderate Shuffle ♩ = 119

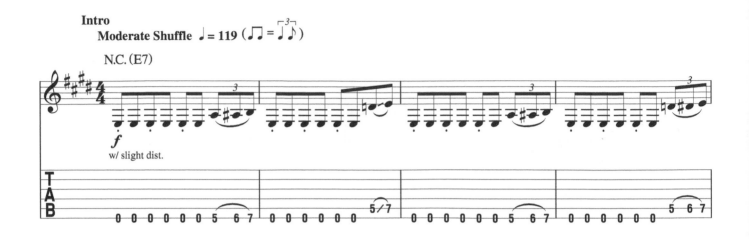

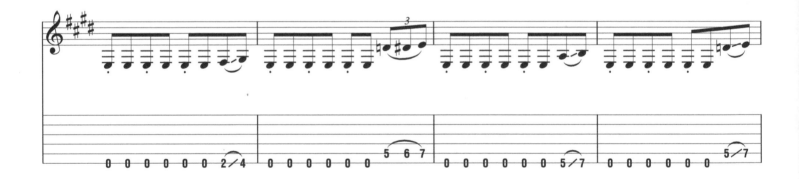

1. A keep your

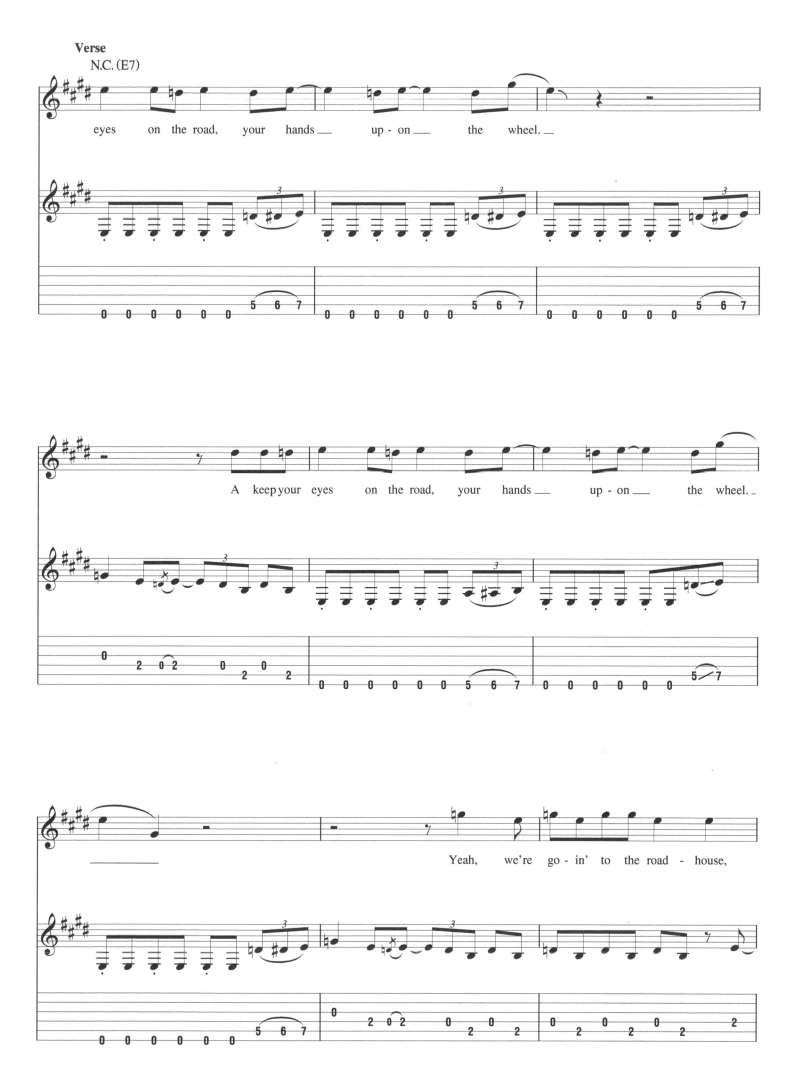

Verse

N.C. (E7)

eyes on the road, your hands ___ up - on ___ the wheel. ___

A keep your eyes on the road, your hands ___ up - on ___ the wheel. ___

___ Yeah, we're go - in' to the road - house,

gon-na have a real, _____ a good time. ____

Interlude

E7

2. Yeah, in

Verse

E7

back of the road - house they got some _ bun - ga - lows. ___

Yeah, in back of the road - house they got some _ bun - ga - lows.

— And that's for the peo - ple who

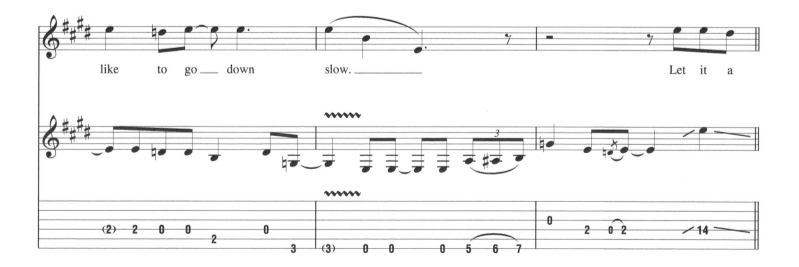

like to go _ down slow. _____ Let it a

Chorus

roll, _____ ba - by, roll. _____ Let it a roll, _____ ba - by, roll. _

slight P.M. -

_____ Let it roll, _____ ba - by, roll. _____ Let it a

slight P.M. - |

Guitar Solo

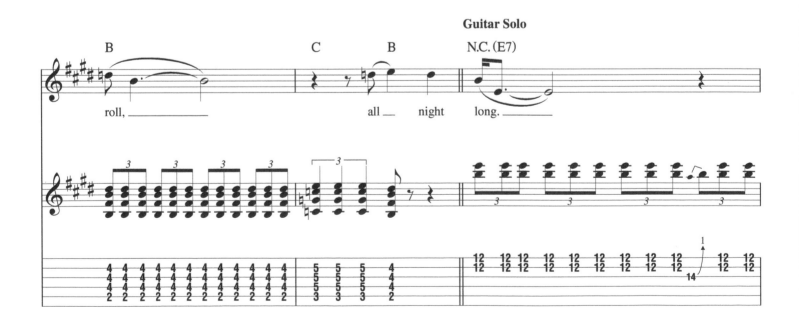

roll, _____ all _ night long. _____

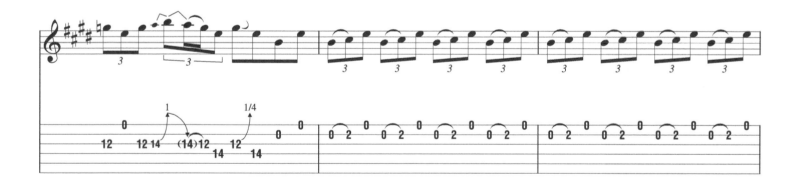

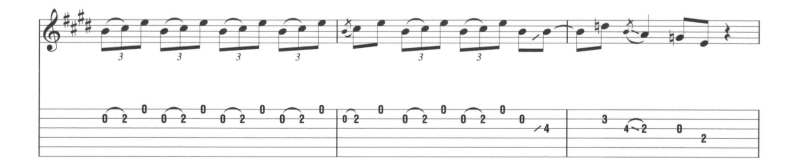

Interlude

N.C. (E7)

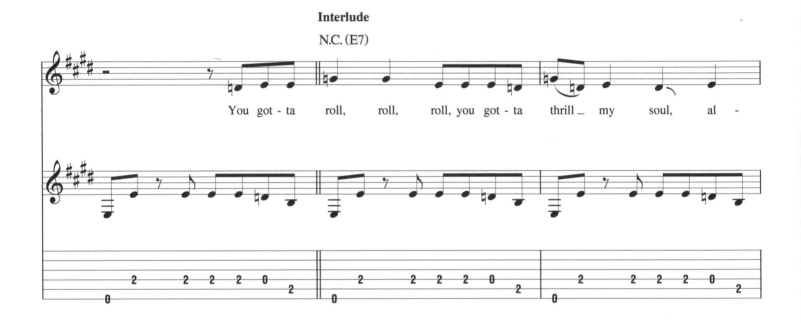

You got-ta roll, roll, roll, you got-ta thrill __ my soul, al -

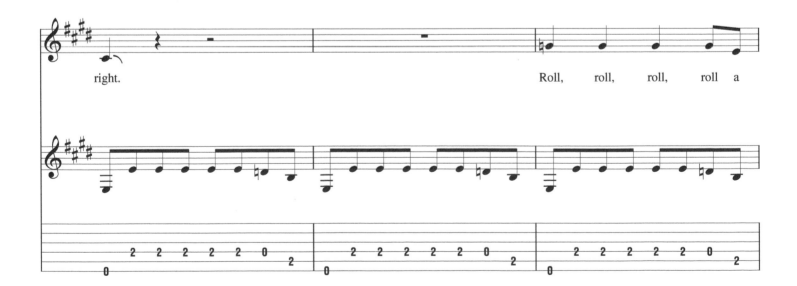

right. Roll, roll, roll, roll a

through my soul __ *de got - ta peep - a con - cha choo - chom, paw conk conk, __ ka - don - ta

*Nonsense syllables

hay - cha coon - a may - cha, ba, ba loo la hey chow, __ bow pa key chow

ee - sown comp, __ yeah, _____ right. _____

Ash - en — la - dy, ash -

- en — la - dy, give up your vows, — give

up your vows. — Save our cit - y, —

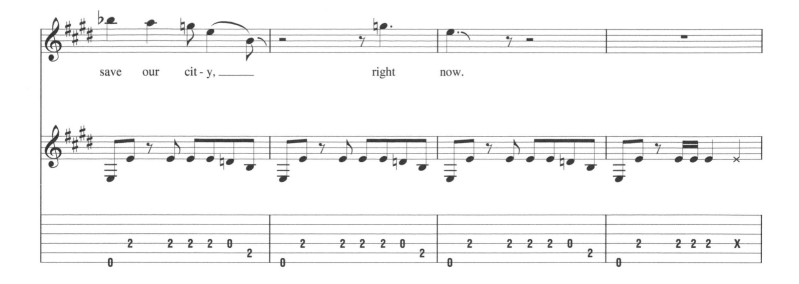

save   our   cit - y, _____   right   now.

Verse

3. When   I   woke up this morn - in'   I

got ___ my - self   a   beer. ___   When   I

woke up this morn - in' __ I got my - self a beer. __

The fu - ture's un - cer - tain and the end is al - ways

Chorus

N.C. (A7)

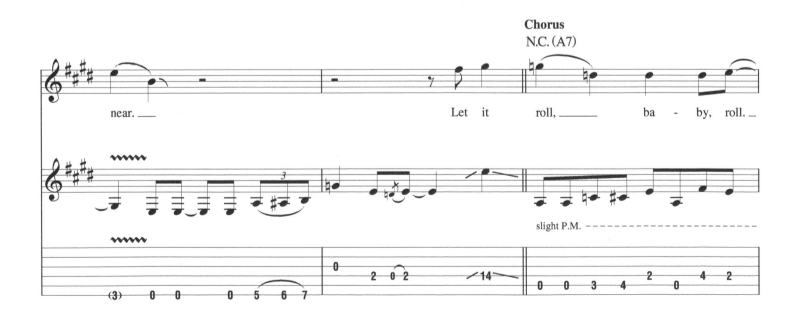

near. __ Let it roll, _____ ba - by, roll. __

slight P.M. - - - - - - - - - - - - - - - - - -

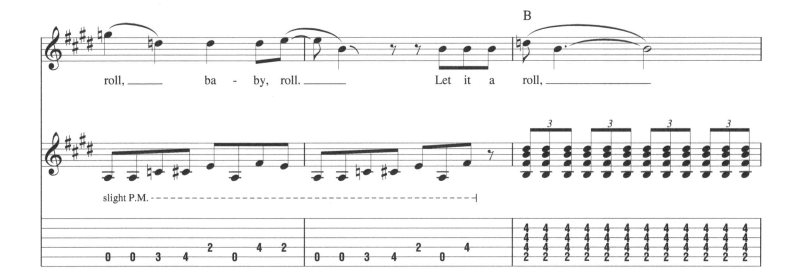

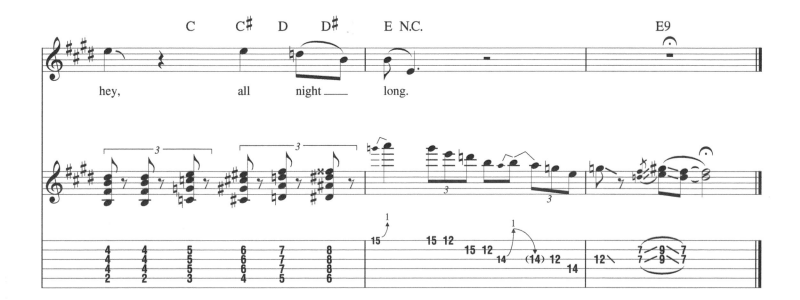

Statesboro Blues

Words and Music by Willy McTell

Open E tuning:
(low to high) E-B-E-G#-B-E

Intro

Moderate shuffle

*Slide positioned halfway
between 13th and 14th fret.

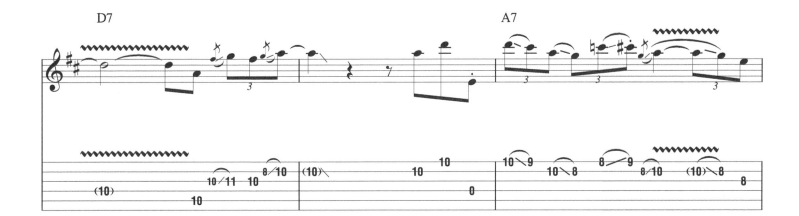

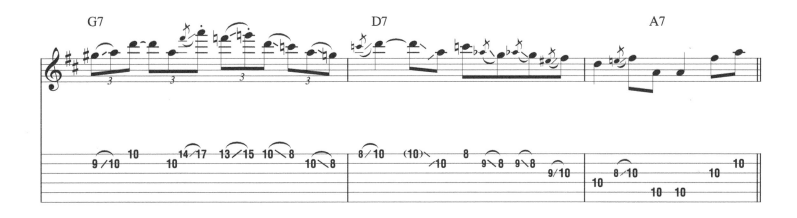

Verse

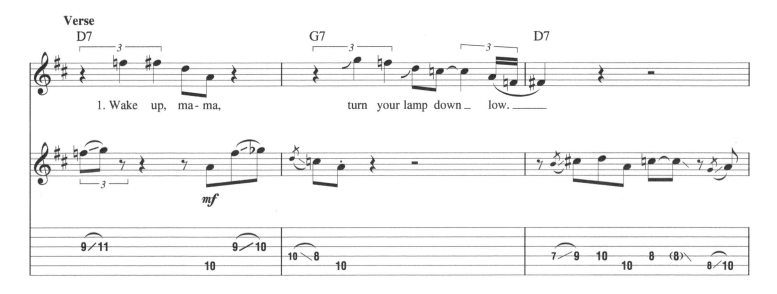

1. Wake up, ma-ma, turn your lamp down___ low. _____

G7

Wake up, ma - ma, turn your lamp down low. _

* Slide positioned halfway
between 8th and 9th fret.

D7   A7

_   Ya got no nerve, _ ba - by,

G7   D7   A7

ya turn Un-cle John from your door. _

Verse

D7   G7   D7

2. I woke _ up this morn - in' an'   I had them States-bo - ro   blues. _

** Slide positioned halfway
between 8th & 9th fret.

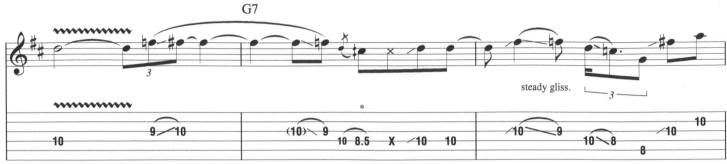

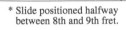

* Slide positioned halfway
between 8th and 9th fret.

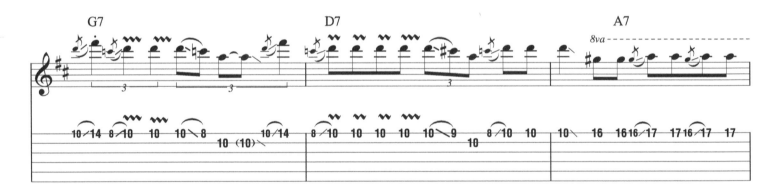

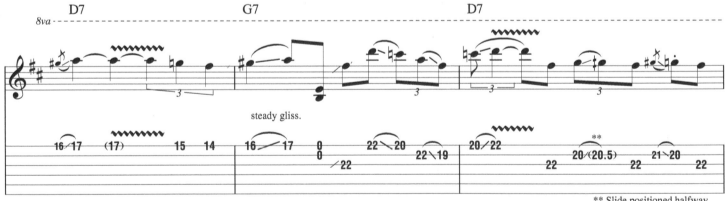

** Slide positioned halfway
between 20th and 21st fret.

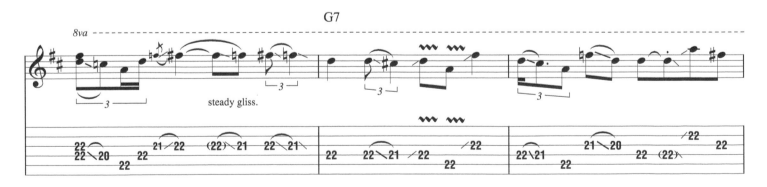

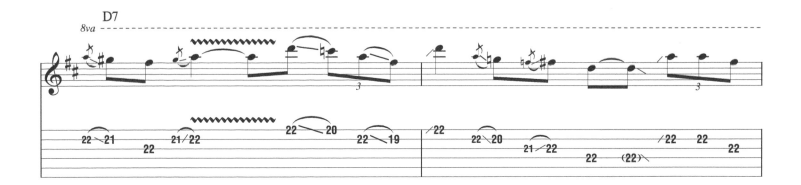

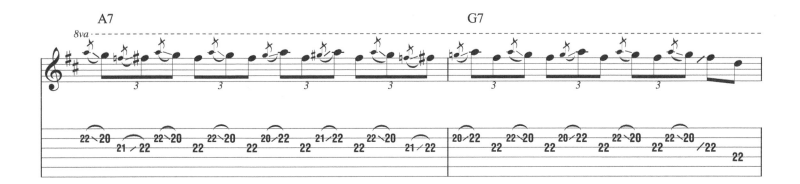

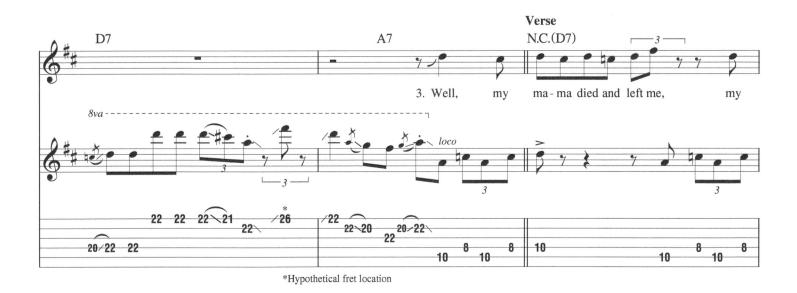

3. Well, my ma-ma died and left me, my

*Hypothetical fret location

pa-pa died and left me. I ain't good look-in', ba - by want some-one sweet and _____ kind. _____

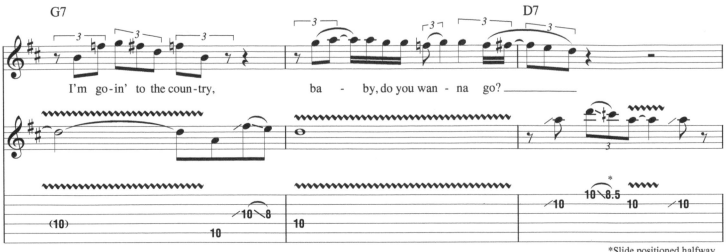

I'm go-in' to the coun-try, ba - by, do you wan - na go? ___

*Slide positioned halfway
between 8th and 9th fret.

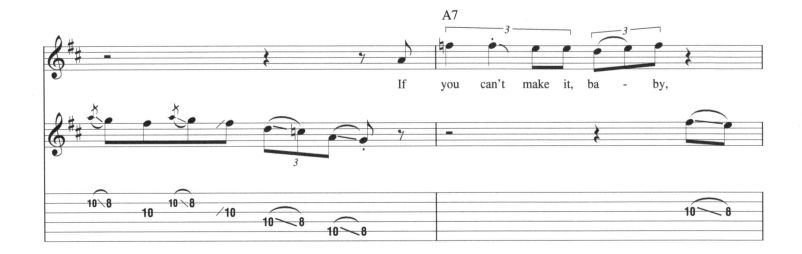

If you can't make it, ba - by,

your sis - ter Lu - cille said she wan-na go. ___ Spoken: Well, I sho' nuff tell ya...

*Sung as even eighth notes.

**Slide positioned halfway
between 8th and 9th fret.

Guitar Solo

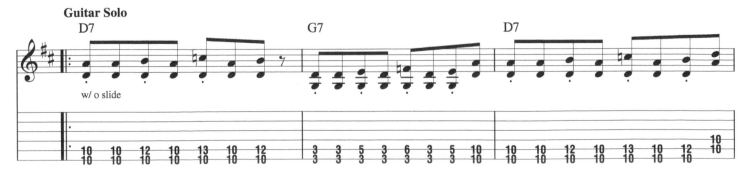

w/o slide

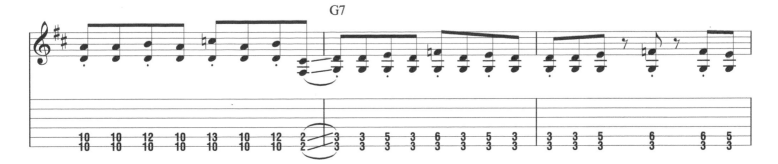

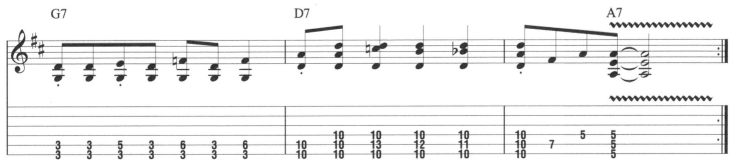

Verse

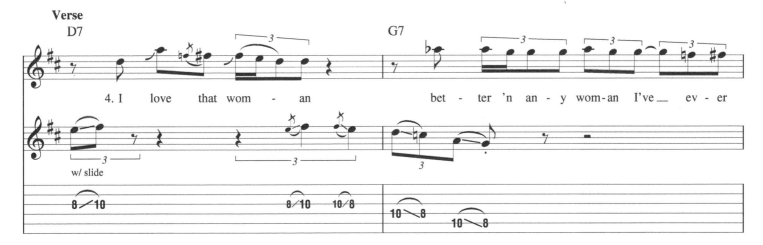

4. I love that wom - an bet - ter 'n an - y wom-an I've __ ev - er

seen. __

Well, I _____ love that wom - an,

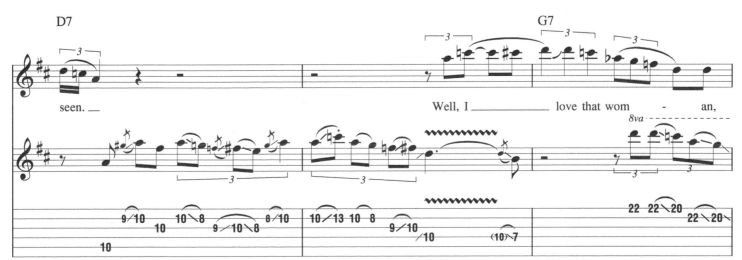

bet - ter 'n an - y wom-an I've_ ev - er seen.

*Slide positioned
halfway between
8th & 9th fret.

Well, she treat me like a king, _ yeah, yeah, yeah, _ I treat her like a dog -

gone queen. _____ 5. Well, _____

Verse

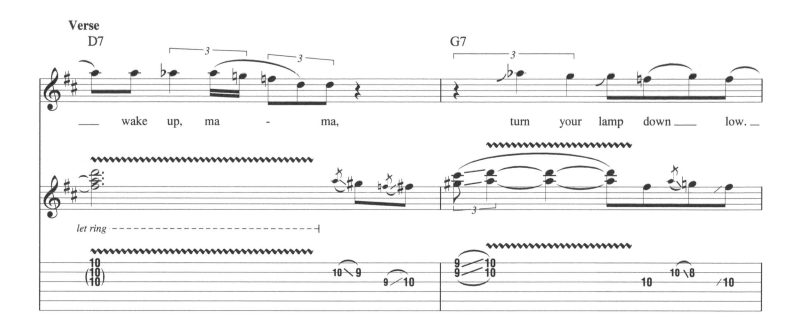

wake up, ma - ma, turn your lamp down ___ low. ___

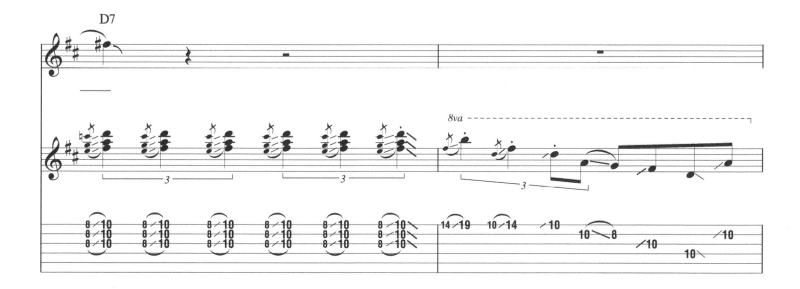

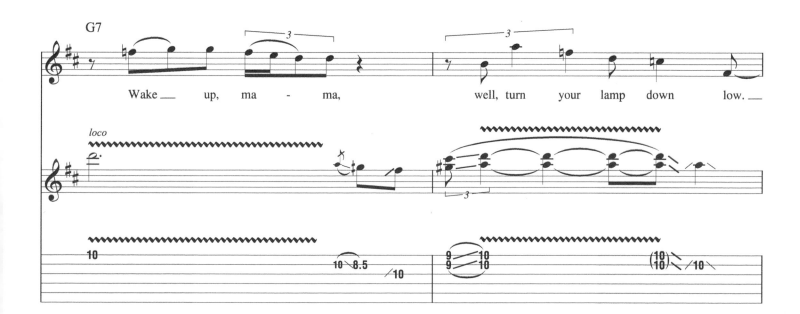

Wake ___ up, ma - ma, well, turn your lamp down low. ___

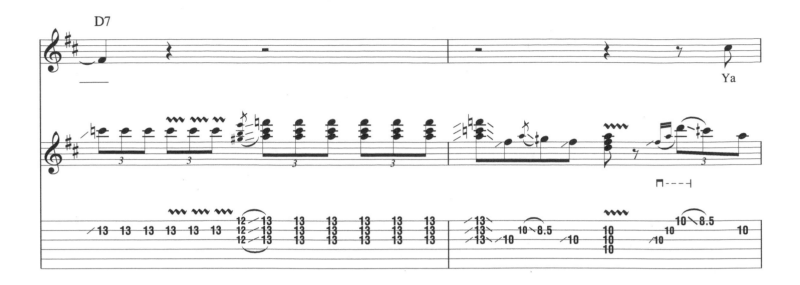

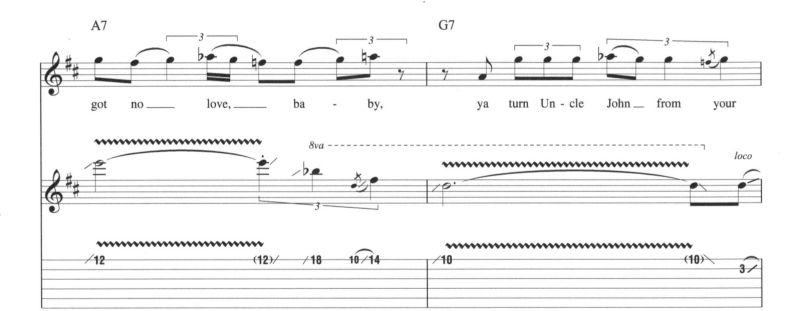

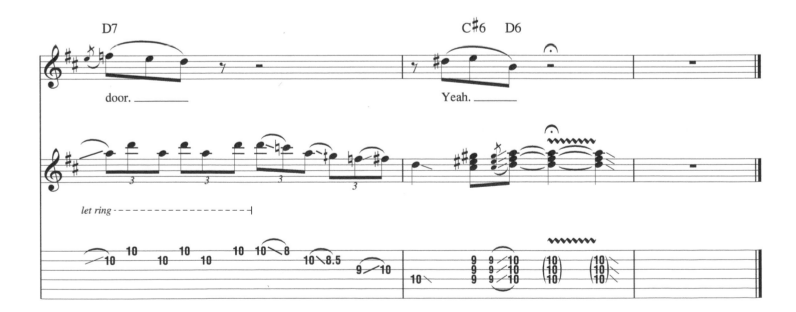